fork me, spoon me

fork me, spoon me

the sensual cookbook

amy reiley

illustrated by kersti frigell

life of reiley

Dedication
To T... and A

Limited edition 2010
ISBN: 978-0-9774120-1-3

art direction and design: Deborah Daly
illustrations: Kersti Frigell
cover photography: Luther Gerlach
conceptual editor and protector of good taste: Ronie Reiley
copy editors: Kristin Voit, Melissa Wilbanks
test kitchen director: Daisie Armstrong

contributing chefs and tastemakers: Daisie Armstrong, Tony Abou-Ganim, Todd Bellucci, Sondra Bernstein, James Corwell, Liz Dueland, Ivy Haaks, Stephan Juliusburger, Nitzi Rabin, Annette Tomei, Neil Wigglesworth

suppliers of wine and spirits fueling test kitchen staff: Ian Blackburn, Michael Cardenas, Greg LaFollette, Lisa Peju, Gran Centenario and Versinthe

special thanks: Arlene Winnick, Dennis Hayes, Dave Reiley, Vik Seshadri, Lark Ellen Gould and all those who loaned their tongues, opinions and hormones. No taste buds were harmed in the making of this book.

PRINTED IN THE UNITED STATES OF AMERICA

table of contents

introduction

Once a man I dated two or three times offered to cook for me. Because I'm involved in the food business, most men never work up the nerve to make me a meal. I was impressed by the boldness of his invitation. And yes, I was pretty doubtful about his cooking skills. But worry was overshadowed by my interest in what was clearly an open invitation to seduction. Any man who invites you over to dinner on the third date has more than whipping soufflé on his mind.

The meal was delicious, the mood electric. There was a white fish in a mango sauce, chocolate, white wine, red wine, and strong cups of coffee that carried us deep into the night.

It was not until much later that he found the nerve to admit he had tried the ambitious menu for the very first time on that night. He chose the ingredients not to showcase his favorite recipes, but because a buddy instructed him to use all the "right" ingredients to create an aphrodisiac dinner.

Although I wish I could claim it, this story is not my own. A magazine food editor I know shared this tale of seduction with me when I started talking about writing *Fork Me*. As a matter of fact, talking about this project provoked an avalanche of ideas and commentary from almost every person in my life. By the way, the pair from the dinner date story married about a year after the mango and chocolate-laden feast.

Fueled by stories like the one shared above, *Fork Me, Spoon Me* grew from a simple idea and took on a life of its own. At its core is a philosophy that eating is a multi-sensory experience, and when combined with the right ingredients and intentions, food becomes positively sexual.

There are many books available to aid in culinary technique, and a few exceptional works have been published to promote sexual satisfaction. It is well documented that the two marry to make the ultimate feast. We've seen it in films from *Like Water for Chocolate* to *9 1/2 Weeks*. The goal of *Fork Me, Spoon Me* is to invite you into a world in which food possesses the power of extraordinary sensuality on its own, or as a prelude to unparalleled bliss.

The structure of *Fork Me, Spoon Me* was inspired by the ultimate "cookbook" for sensuality, *The Joy of Sex*. Arguably the most successful sexual self-help book ever published, *The Joy of Sex* capitalized on the sensory pleasures of food. And

introduction

yet, no cookbook has yet to nibble on this titillating topic by inspiring and celebrating culinary experimentation and the sensual pleasure that *The Joy of Sex* first brought to life decades ago.

When I started on the book, I realized that my topic can be broken down into identical categories to those in *The Joy of Sex*, although, in the end, I made a couple of minor adjustments: I've added a category of libations along with a sauce chapter because the class of liquid pleasure is far too profound to be limited only to those compounds you can drizzle over meat. I've also included a chapter on desserts, which was superfluous to *Sex* since that book's every chapter was nothing but dessert. What can I say? I've got an insatiable sweet tooth.

Fork Me, Spoon Me, like *The Joy of Sex*, is meant to be a menu, not a rule book. It is impossible to write with passion about things you do not enjoy, so I've included recipes that embody the way I like to eat. You may have your own method for incorporating these arousing ingredients into food-inspired foreplay. In the world of aphrodisiac foods, experimentation is encouraged!

introduction

the moods of food

Although countless foods have been declared aphrodisiacs at some point in history, I wanted to feature aphrodisiac ingredients with both folkloric history and scientific evidence supporting their arousing abilities. I've selected twelve of my all-time favorite aphrodisiac ingredients to share with you in these pages.

Eat Mangoes Naked is the title of a book by one of my favorite authors, Sark. The work focuses on achieving creative freedom and describes how eating mangoes naked can inspire a woman to experience freedom in every corner of her life.

"No woman should go a day without chocolate!" These are words of wisdom my mother drilled into me since childhood. For her, chocolate provides that break from the bonds of social conformity that Sark imagined mangoes could elicit.

"I could give up every food but figs," are the words from the lips of a friend whose love for the sensual fruit's shape is very much at the heart of the inspiration of this book.

Every woman I talk to has a different relationship with these ingredients, but the one similarity I have found is that the bond each woman has with her favorite ingredient has more to do with emotion and physical effects than with flavor.

introduction

what's in a name

I chose the title *Fork Me, Spoon Me* because I wanted a name that both embodied the book's central concept and captured each ingredient's sensuous spirit.

As I experimented with my chosen ingredients, I began to form unique bonds with every one of them. I discovered that each ingredient brought out a different side of my personality and that I can choose ingredients that change my mood and enhance whatever style of seductress I want to become.

The ingredients featured in this book only scratch the surface of what I suspect can be achieved with aphrodisiac foods. I firmly believe that it is not so much the ingredient alone, but rather the intention with which you eat it, the willingness to give yourself over to the creative experience of cooking and eating, and, sometimes most importantly, the setting you create in which to share your feast.

kiss

Keep it simple, sexpot. I've tried to incorporate recipes into each chapter that require minimum effort for maximum impact. When using the seductive qualities of food, I always prefer following instructions that give my hands as much free time as possible.

Several of the recipes in this book were created by noted American chefs whose cooking lends itself to culinary seduction. Although their recipes tend to require a little more expertise to prepare, I felt it was important not only to add some variety to the book's overriding style, but to introduce readers to different approaches and philosophies of seductive cuisine. I think it is the male perspectives in particular that bring a healthy counterbalance to my feminine wiles.

introduction

ingredients

almond

Almond is the world's most popular member of the nut family. Although its mythical aphrodisiac history is woven through the stories of ancient Greece and Rome, today it's also extremely popular as a romantic lure in the Far East.

Around the world, the blossoms of the almond tree are considered to be harbingers of spring, new life and the blooming of love. Matured on the tree, the fruit becomes the perfect symbol of autumn, the season during which almonds are harvested. Removed from its shell and roasted, the nut's sweet meat has an alluring hint of sweetness in any season.

Almonds are an international symbol of fertility and are considered to be an essential sexual element in Arabic pastries. They are served as a prelude to a meal in many Mediterranean cultures where natives suggest that the almond's scent will drive women wild.

serving almonds

I will never forget the first time I tasted green almonds, the fresh fruit of the almond tree, picked young and presented still in its gray-green casing. The exotic fruit was served in one of my favorite California restaurants as an accompaniment to cheese. I was instructed to carefully cut away the greenish hull, which revealed the ivory pearl housed within—the sweet, immature almond meat.

The work required to remove the delicious core from its protective shell makes eating almonds much more than a way to stave off hunger. It is an experience in which to indulge and it doesn't have to be with a green almond—I feel the same about the more common hard-shelled nuts.

Honestly, I love almonds even when they're crushed in baklava or served shelled in an earthen bowl accompanied by a glass of French rosé wine. To me, almonds are the most stimulating variety of nut, slightly bitter but still sweet meat that makes an almost celebratory "pop" when it's crunched.

ingredients

chile

Chile is like the hard-core drug of the culinary world. When you slip it into a dish, it can bring an immediate, full-on flush. Used in the right proportion, it's guaranteed to make your heart pound just a little more quickly.

Chile has dazzled daring diners and medicine men from Thailand to Tahiti to Brazil. In Africa, it's been added to bathing water as a beauty aide. In Samoa, it's blended into Kava, the notorious potion of love and virility. Chile's abilities to raise body temperature and make tongues

ingredients

tingle and lips plump are adored the world over in the games of love. In Mexico, it's boiled in broth as a hangover cure. In Bolivia, it's blended in cocaine for a serious rush. In the Southwest, its antidote is tequila, which, I can promise from experience, will ease that pain.

hot for chile

About one in four people is born with an extremely high proportion of taste buds. Some scientists estimate they may have as many as four times the norm (inexplicably, the majority of these "supertasters" are women). For supertasters, even a hint of chile can overwhelm the senses. I am a supertaster.

But for me, the force with which chile assaults my sense of taste is no turn-off. In fact, I think the flush of heat helps to heighten chile's allure. Since chile's aphrodisiac impact is to awaken the senses and raise body heat, I am the ultimate lightweight, powerless in its clutches. This is not to say that chile's aphrodisiac effects are diminished in those with a normal number of taste buds—they are not. And for this I consider this fiery redhead the most brazen of spices.

ingredients

chocolate

Chocolate is the gastronomic Helen of Troy, the most powerful object of culinary affection ever desired. It held the Marquis de Sade in a powerful embrace, and Napoleon, as well. But it was Montezuma who best understood how to harness chocolate's prowess. The ancient ruler apparently drank a ritual 50 cups of chocolate before entertaining his harem each and every day.

Chocolate is as tempting to women as to men, as was observed by Casanova. It seems that the Latin lover knew how to charm the ladies with his stash.

Many claim that chocolate's magnetism is more scientific than psychological, since chocolate contains stimulants similar to caffeine as well as to the euphoria-inducing compounds serotonin and phenylethylamine. But naysayers claim that these drugs are present in doses far too small to make a measurable difference in mood.

No matter what the true secret to its lure, chocolate is such a powerful temptation that it has been banned by governments, smuggled under the covers, and even traded as the most valuable of currencies. A rich, sweet midnight kiss, chocolate is a bite for serious lovers.

ingredients

nibbling chocolate

It is my mother's firm belief that chocolate, not diamonds, is a woman's true best friend.

Although I don't share my mother's need for a daily hit of the sweet stuff, I do know that even the smallest nibble of melting, creamy chocolate can lull my taste buds into a state of complete ecstasy. And in my meanderings into aphrodisiac field research, I've concluded that dense, chocolate brownies, not oysters, whipped cream or any of the other clichés, are without a doubt my ultimate aphrodisiac food.

ingredients

fig

Split down the center and cradled by a palm, the fig's pink flesh is said to resemble a woman's most personal parts. For this reason, it is believed that eating a fresh fig while naked in front of a woman is a powerfully erotic act.

The luscious fruit's womanly wiles were immortalized in the words of author D. H. Lawrence who dedicated a poem entitled "Figs" to its sensuality.

The fig is a little like a shy girl making only a brief appearance during the height of summer. A delicate fruit, it unfortunately does not travel well. The fig is usually found close to home—a freshly picked delicacy for the lucky few.

Some suspect that the fig's original home was the Garden of Eden. And some historians claim the fig was the original temptress, the true forbidden fruit.

But even those who still cling to the myth of the apple find the fig's charms to be undeniable. This soft, plump fruit is a fine source of iron and potassium—minerals much needed in the horizontal pas de deux.

ingredients

celebrating figs

If it were not for the soft, plump flesh of the fig, this book would not exist.

Early in my career in food and wine, a very close friend and respected colleague shared with me her obsession with the aphrodisiac properties of figs. Together, we thumbed countless pages of research and folklore on this single topic. I could not believe how much had been written through the ages on the sensuality of a sole ingredient. For me, this awakening was the beginning of what I hope will be a lifetime of work discovering the sensual pleasures derived from foods around the globe.

The friend who introduced me to the world of sensual foods was one of the hottest mamas I've ever known. That a woman so deliciously self-empowered to celebrate sensuality to its fullest could be captivated by the arousing power of one tiny fruit led me to believe that figs are indeed gifts of great mystery and temptation.

ingredients

ginger

Ginger makes a girl feel naughty but nice (think giggling Geisha). This little exotic spice can make even the most jaded food lover blush, thanks to its ability to raise body heat. Ginger also promises to make the tongue tingle and lips swell. (It recently gained popularity as the irritant in "plumping" glosses, those lipsticks promising to make lips both glossily moist and swollen. If you've never had a close encounter with this kind of gloss, put "kissing with lips swabbed by plumping gloss" on your list of 1,000 things to do before you die.)

Ginger's been exciting tongues in the Far East since prerecorded history. Fresh ginger is an affordable little nugget tucked in the corner of the

ingredients

produce isle. In India, it's juiced and mixed with eggs and a touch of honey to cure impotence. In days of yore, European maidens devoured ginger-bread men as a ritual that was supposed to bring them husbands and a quick end to premarital chastity.

Folklore aside, ginger's ability to increase circulation is a powerful plus in making my favorite Japanese dish, "horizontal sushi." And, speaking of Japanese, ginger has a natural affinity for sake.

Play with ginger raw, pounded, pickled, and of course, candied. Any way you slice it, this little root will warm you to your core.

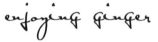

enjoying ginger

As a child, I never liked ginger. My parents would feed me chunks of candied ginger to treat an upset stomach, and I hated every stinging bite. As I grew older I began to discover the difference between "good" and "bad" pain, and I realized that ginger hurts so good. I love the sweet sting it brings to Asian and modern American dishes and the effect eating ginger has on my body. I love the way my lips tingle and my cheeks flush, even after the merest slice.

ingredients

honey

Liquid pleasure, honey is an incurably addictive sweetener with as many styles as wine. From full-bodied to outright spicy, its varied flavors inspire chefs around the world. Honey's powers mostly manifest as a quick shot of sugar-fed energy, but its hypnotic secret is its appeal to the human longing for sweetness. A spoonful of deliciously thick honey spread on butter-drenched toast awakens the senses. But it is even more alluring when drizzled on fingers or licked from toes.

ingredients

In Eastern Europe, a spoonful of this golden succulence is poured into the palms of bridal couples. Licking honey's sweet goodness from one another's hands, the newly wedded pair is supposed to discover tender caresses with which they will touch each other forevermore.

Transforming honey into alcoholic mead earns the viscous liquid a starring role in ritual intoxication. In the Middle Ages, wedding couples indulged in a long, slow drink of honey mead every day for the first month of marriage—it is from this rite that we get the word honeymoon.

Languid, silky and alluringly sticky, honey is a temptress of worldwide appeal.

serving honey

Honey makes me feel as sweet as dessert and as sensual as a leopard on the prowl. I adore this elixir licked straight from the jar.

Pulling the jar of honey out of the cupboard is like playtime. Watching golden streams drizzle from a spoon is nearly hypnotic.

 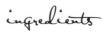

mango

Throughout history, the Southeast Asian royalty kept mango groves as symbols of status and offered the "perfect" mangoes as gifts of the highest order. In this, as well as other tropical cultures, mangoes are linked with male sexuality because they are considered to resemble the shape of a testicle (wishful thinking).

Plump, juicy, and close to bursting from its skin with sweet flesh, the mango at its ripest is almost irresistible, which is the best explanation

I can fathom for the constant recommendation by poets and philosophers. An immeasurable number of romantic texts suggest the succulent fruit to be eaten naked with the sweet, vanilla-scented juice running where it may.

One Indian poet, perhaps the victim of a fermented mango juice OD, took his affair with the ripe fruit so far as to dub whole mangoes as "sealed jars of paradisiacal honey." India, it should be added, is the nation in which men are prescribed mango therapy to increase virility. It is unknown whether there is truth to its properties as a miracle cure or if mango therapy is simply a ploy to bump up mango consumption in the world's leading mango-producing nation.

licking mangoes

I love the ritual involved in serving mangoes. The ripe fruit is a food I like to eat when I'm in a languishing mood, taking the time to experience every individual second of the seduction. Removing the skin takes dexterity and care—it simply cannot be rushed. While slicing the meat away from the pit, I love the feel of sweet, orange mango juice running down my arm. And I never discard the pit. Sucking every last bit of sweetness from the tough core is the most rewarding part of this performance.

mint

Shakespeare immortalized mint's power to seduce by recommending this fresh, sweet herb as a natural Viagra for middle-aged men.

Mint is grown all over the world for culinary and medicinal use. Chefs in countries as diverse as France, Turkey, India, Portugal, Cuba and Thailand love to tease their dishes with its fresh kiss. As great chefs the world over know but few home cooks realize, mint comes in enough varieties to suit whatever your style of seduction. If you like a strong come-on try peppermint. Or try apple mint for something gentle and sweet.

Mint can multiply faster than a fertile jackrabbit. And it fills out gardens with fresh-scented foliage as proficiently as Marilyn Monroe could fill out a halter dress. Used in combination with other aphrodisiac ingredients, mint is the component noted for increasing appetites of all kinds. Just one quick nibble, and it will leave your breath as fresh as a bedtime brushing.

Cool, complex and every bit elegant, mint can be a perfect fit for cooks of every shape and size.

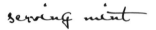

I run out into my garden and pull a few mint sprigs to use in my cooking for those intensely hot interludes that need a cooling influence. Scientific studies demonstrate that women find mint-fragranced breath alluring, but in my own unscientific observations, I conclude that it goes both ways.

ingredients

peach

Picked warm from the tree, this Southern belle's sun-kissed flesh is considered reminiscent of a woman's curves.

In *A Midsummer Nights' Dream,* the fairies passed around plump peach flesh as a symbol of temptation. (Remember that this is a story in which the fairies' romantic powers inspired interspecies pairing!)

The ancient Chinese believed the juicy flesh bursting from the peach's lightly fuzzed skin held magical properties. In Japan, blushing brides hold peach blossoms in celebration of fertility. Poet William Fahey compared the ripe, clefted, pink

ingredients

fruits to the plunge of cleavage so studied in the paintings of the French Impressionist, Renoir.

But the peach's finest attributes are actually in its kiss, so to speak. Packed with vitamins and primary nutrients, peaches offer potassium, phosphorus, iron, A and C—all key ingredients in performance enhancement.

petting peaches

A simple, ripe peach makes for a spectacularly multisensory eating experience. With skin so soft, it could be velvet and with a color like pale skin flushed from exertion, this soft, summer fruit is quite simply sexy. But to catch a peach at flavorful perfection takes patience and persistence. Seek out only those peaches with a pure, unmarked skin and flesh that gives ever-so-slightly when squeezed against the palm. This is essential.

And yes, I've been caught more than once in the produce aisle idly petting the peaches.

rosemary

An old-fashioned beauty, rosemary has been used throughout the ages to bring focus and clarity, for protection and in the cleansing of sacred spaces. Shakespeare's Ophelia used rosemary as a symbol of remembrance.

Rosemary is incorporated into medicines to reduce inflammation and stimulate digestion. But this sweet, herbal beauty is noted for stimulating much more than the digestive system. Its flavors and aromas are considered invigorating, energizing and inspiring.

Popular in peasant foods in the lusty south of France and Spain, rosemary has a direct, herbal taste that brings a focused intensity to dishes that carries through any evening spent in its sweet embrace.

relishing rosemary

Rosemary is among my favorite herbs. I have three varieties growing in my garden. One has a slightly lemony flavor. Another produces the most beautiful, tiny, blue flowers. The third is my favorite for cooking because its slightly soft, green leaves impart the classic rosemary flavor.

Something about the aroma of rosemary seems to belong in another era, as though it were an ingredient favored by the lovelorn women of Victorian novels. I like using rosemary in timeless, comforting dishes, including some from Victorian times. For me rosemary evokes a sense of security and calm wrapped in a delectably fragrant package.

saffron

Like a Persian Queen, saffron is a rare Eastern beauty. But its aphrodisiac allure, according to the Knights of Arabia who used this elusive sorceress with judicious wisdom, is believed to be most effective on women. However, ancient Persian women found a use for saffron that was effective in attracting men: as a stain on the skin to mimic a sun-kissed glow.

ingredients

The Romans adopted both viewpoints and used saffron to scent baths of both aristocratic gentlemen and their female lovers.

It is hard not to be wild about saffron, though its love comes at a price. The most rare and expensive spice in the world, saffron is sought for its brilliant color, which stains everything it touches with a shade of sunlight gold.

Its slightly bitter, herbal taste and stunning hue dominate in the cuisines of the Middle East, but its allure crosses cultures into the foods and lifestyle of Europe's glamorous Mediterranean coast.

selecting saffron

Saffron is a hard spice to work with because its flavor is subtle, almost to the point of imperception. I use this rare spice when I want a strong splash of color.

If saffron were a woman, she would have a split personality. In the actual prep of a dish she's a dominatrix, coloring everything she touches (including your hands if you share my naughty habit of sticking your fingers in everything) with a glowing gold. But once she reaches the dining table, she becomes submissive, allowing stronger flavors to dominate and often overpower her subtle advances.

vanilla

An exotic beauty propagating strictly in tropical locales, vanilla was first brought to the "civilized" world by Cortez. He, no doubt, had observed its aphrodisiac powers in action on the Aztec ruler Montezuma who daily entertained a harem of fifty.

In scientific studies on scent, the arousing aroma of vanilla has proven to be a strong temptation to men of all ages. And although much of the research on vanilla's provoking powers has surfaced in recent years, even as far back as the eighteenth century its powers were applied to the problem of lagging libido. In a German study in 1762, medicines based on vanilla extract were found to have a 100% success rate for curing impotence.

Don't be fooled by imposters; there are many synthetic imitations of vanilla's pure extract of love on the market, which are sold as "vanilla flavor." Although these imposters can capture the aroma's most dominant note, they lack the captivating complexity of perfume and flavors that make real vanilla the erotic exotic we love.

ingredients

loving vanilla

For me, vanilla is the spice to be brought out in winter. The warmth of its aroma and flavor generates body heat. What better inspiration for a little indoor sport?

There's something about vanilla's scent that is so comforting. It can lull me into a sense of security even when I've hit the brick wall of stress. And relaxation is known to be a key for shedding inhibition. Simmering a vanilla bean on the stove in a pot of water is an essential element in the shy girl's arsenal.

ingredients

starters

hot honey nuts
chile

figs in a blanket
figs

first time fluffernutters
chocolate

rosemary biscotti bites
rosemary

shrimp-stuffed spring rolls
mint

honey-almond home cured snapper
almond

zucchini stuffed with warm lobster
vanilla

peach lover's summer gazpacho
peach

honey carrot soup
honey

hot honey nuts

Nuts are superfoods when it comes to enhancing sexual health. Many varieties of nuts contain high concentrations of zinc, which is essential for blood flow. And, of course, nuts are a primary source of protein. If you reach back into your brain for that little nugget from seventh grade health class, you'll recall that protein is the building block of energy. (And who said middle school was a waste of time?)

preparation

1/4 c honey
2 c mixed nuts
1 T butter
1/2 t dried chile flakes

Preheat oven to 350 degrees.

Melt butter in a small saucepan while slowly dribbling honey with the chile flakes into the steamy pot. Boil gently for 2 minutes, being careful not to scorch your honey.

Pour honey over your nuts on a foil-lined baking sheet. Fold up the edges of the foil to prevent your sweet honey from oozing all over the oven. *(Warning:* The honey mixture will be very hot. Do not touch anything with your hands or you'll find yourself sucking your own finger the rest of the night.)

Roast in oven for 8-10 minutes and flip nuts halfway through. Take your nuts from the tray and allow them to cool for 20 minutes before eating. Clean the tray immediately or the sticky residue will be with you forever.

Variation on a theme: For a cool version of honey nuts, try swapping one teaspoon dried lavender in place of the chile flakes. Lavender blossoms are noted for their relaxing effects. Although they are often used to improve sleep, they're also excellent for relaxing muscles and reducing inhibitions.

the art of eating nuts

It's all in the technique. No need to practice. Think slow, sexy and purposeful. Lick off the spice, suck on the sugar and tease the residue from your fingers with the tip of your tongue.

starters

figs in a blanket

Sadly, the research leads us to no conclusions on the aphrodisiac effects of prosciutto, or of pork in general. But as legends go, the succulent meat of every variety—from boar to sow—is intertwined with the lore of seduction. The great temptress Cleopatra was known to have a pig roasting for Anthony at every hour of the day and night. What man doesn't want pork on return from a long trip?

preparation

4 fresh figs, halved*
8 thin strips prosciutto

*Green, Kadota figs are excellent for this recipe because they have thick skins and are easier to grill than some fig varieties. But any ripe, summer fig works in my book.

Coat grill rack with oil and heat to a medium temperature.

Envelop each of the 8 fig halves in prosciutto meat.

Drop the fig parcels on the hot grill and cook for 5 minutes. Flip parcels halfway through. Serve warm as finger food.

In winter, cook figs under the oven broiler to save yourself from shriveling in the snow

Although I can't feed you hard facts on the aphrodisiac properties of prosciutto, I do know that this salty pork works a certain gastronomical magic when it envelops a fig. When grilled together, the salt and fat of the meat almost melts into the fig's soft flesh, promising a medley of savory and sweet, crisped edges that lead to a velvety, warm center.

first time fluffernutters

When I initially committed to writing *Fork Me, Spoon Me*, I wanted the recipes to include really unique creations. So I invited a number of friends to my house, lined up about every sandwich-making ingredient I could think of, fired up the panini maker, and challenged everyone to a sandwich-making contest. And I sweetened the deal with the promise that the winner's recipe was to be featured in the upcoming book.

True to my word, I am sharing the blue ribbon combination. But I can't credit it to just one cook. The truth of the matter is that at least half

starters

the guests swiped their bread with an identical pairing: a wickedly decadent twist on a childhood sweet, the fluffernutter. I dubbed the sandwich the "first time fluffernutter," not because its sweet amalgamation of flavors promises to spin young love out of control (although it might), but because the combination is packed with such a sinfully sweet, bitter, nutty, gooey harmony of flavors that even a veteran fluffernutterer will know that they are truly experiencing fluffernutters for the very first time.

1 T chocolate-flavored
    peanut butter
1 1/2 T marshmallow
    fluff*
2 slices seeded, whole
    grain bread
1/2 T salted butter

*My fluff of choice is Ricemallow, a more natural and slightly less sweet mixture, devoid of some of the original's most likely toxic ingredients.

preparation

Heat a sandwich press. (If you don't have a sandwich press, heat a small frying pan over medium heat.)

Butter the outside of both slices of bread. Spread the inside of one slice with the chocolate peanut butter, the other with I 1 T of fluff. Form a sandwich and press until the outside is toasted to golden. If you are using a frying pan, press the sandwich with a large spatula. When one side is golden, flip and repeat. Top the hot sandwich with an additional 1/2 T marshmallow fluff. Cut your crispy, toasted sandwich into quarters and serve with extra napkins.

a couple that fluffernutters together...

Two friends from the abovementioned sandwich party, who are separately charming but together a magical pairing, have been among this sandwich's most vocal supporters. And although I don't think Arlene and Richard really need nutter butter to bind their unbreakable union, the passion they have shared bringing this simple recipe to the perfect state of sweet, gooey warmth is something we all hope to experience.

rosemary biscotti bites

Biscotti stands for "cookie" in Italian, although the word more accurately translates to "twice baked."

The most familiar biscotti are sweet cookies with a shelf life of several months. This savory version will last only about a week thanks to the perishable aspect of its main ingredient: sharp, Italian cheese. But it's that cheesy filling that gives these mini morsels their ultra-aphrodisiac impact. Cheese contains PEA, (phenylethylamine), a potent, naturally occurring mood enhancer. Eating

2 c flour
1 t baking powder
pinch sea salt
1 t sugar
1 1/2 T fresh rosemary,
    chopped
1/3 c buttermilk
2 T butter, melted
2 eggs
1 c Parmesan, shredded*
vegetable cooking spray

*The quality of the biscotti is directly impacted by the quality of the cheese. I highly recommend investing in a good, aged Parm. However, if you do use an artisan cheese, you may need to add a little extra salt, since aged, artisan cheeses tend to contain less salt than their factory-made counterparts. For a more pungent flavor, try using aged Pecorino instead of Parmesan.

cheese is believed to release a surge of hormones almost identical to that of sexual climax.

preparation

Preheat oven to 350 degrees.

Mix flour, baking powder, salt, sugar, and rosemary in a large bowl.

Combine buttermilk, butter, and eggs in a small bowl; whip with a wire whisk. Stir in cheese. Then add liquid ingredients to flour mixture, while stirring to make a crumbly dough.

Turn the dough out onto a lightly floured surface and knead with a light touch 7 or 8 times. Shape dough into a thin log about 16 inches long. Place your log on a baking sheet coated with cooking spray and flatten the top of the roll to a 1-inch thickness.

Bake log at 350 degrees for 30 minutes. Move log from baking sheet to a wire rack and cool for 10 minutes. Cut log on the diagonal into 24 biscotti-shaped slices. Put biscotti cookies back on the baking sheet. Reduce oven temperature to 325 degrees and bake 15 minutes. Turn your cookies over and bake an additional 15 minutes (biscotti will be slightly soft in center but will harden as they cool). Remove from baking sheet; let cool completely on wire rack.

Note: if your oven runs hot, consider cooking the sliced biscotti at 300 degrees for 15 minutes per side. If you notice the biscotti turning brown after the first 15 minutes of cooking, turn down the oven before the backside gets burned.

my favorite cookie

Nothing beats good biscotti. How can you not love slender, hard cookies that never go soft and rarely turn stale? And these biscotti tip the sexy scale even further with their stuffing of tangy, Italian cheese, a food known for releasing a rush of happy hormones. I like to keep these rosemary-perfumed cookies around for midnight munchies.

shrimp-stuffed spring rolls

by Annette Tomei, private chef and wine country vixen

1/2 oz dried glass noodles or bean thread noodles

1 t rice wine vinegar

1/2 t soy sauce or Tamari

dash of toasted sesame oil

pinch of ground coriander

1/2 carrot, peeled and cut into julienne strips

1/2 red bell pepper cut into julienne strips

4 scallions (green part only) cut into julienne strips

4 6-in rice papers

8 pesticide-free nasturtium flower blossoms

4 large, fresh shrimp, split in half lengthwise

12 fresh mint leaves

1/4 c fresh cilantro leaves

8 fresh basil leaves

Mint brings a taste of freshness to this slippery finger food for two. Naming this prolific herb for a notorious concubine, Mintha, the ancient Greeks considered mint to be warming to the body and perhaps a bit dangerous. Here it is combined with shrimp, a famed aphrodisiac of the sea. As long as you have no qualms about seafood, this pairing of earth and sea should cause enchantment.

You should be warned though, that the process of delicately rolling these Vietnamese morsels is a lengthy labor of love, and the duties are best when shared. When performed with four hands, the electricity of fingers mingling as they slide over the wet spring roll skin is an experience of affection that will make the whole process worthwhile.

preparation

Soak the glass noodles in warm water for 20 minutes. While the noodles bathe, bring a large pot of salted water to a rolling boil.

Before cooking the pasta, prepare a bath of cold water in a large bowl.

Drain wet noodles, then cook for 1 minute in the boiling salted water; transfer immediately to cold-water bath to stop the cooking. Drain well.

In a medium bowl, combine the rice vinegar, soy sauce, sesame oil, and coriander. Toss the julienne of carrot, red bell pepper, and scallions in the dressing.

Arrange a workspace with a bowl of water, a damp cloth to roll on, and each prepped ingredient in a separate bowl. Line a baking sheet with plastic wrap and have ready a damp cotton towel to cover the finished rolls.

Working with one sheet at a time, soak the rice paper in water until it is soft and pliable (up to 30 seconds) and move to the damp towel work surface. Arrange two nasturtiums, face down, in the center of the rice paper and layer 2 shrimp halves on top of the flowers. Arrange three mint leaves, one quarter of the cilantro leaves, two basil leaves, carrots, bell pepper, scallions, and noodles closely together. Fold the sides in onto the filling; carefully roll from top to bottom as tightly as possible, like a delicate, love-laced burrito. Run damp fingers along the edge to smooth the seal. Gently place your mouth-wateringly fat roll seam side down on the baking sheet. Cover with the damp towel and then with plastic wrap. Repeat with the remaining rice paper sheets. Serve immediately with the chile-ginger dip or store in the fridge until serving. Let the rolls warm slightly before devouring.

starters

1 thinly sliced Thai
    chile
1 T chopped fresh ginger
1 T sugar
2 T fish sauce
2 T lime juice
2 T water

FOR THE CHILE-GINGER DIPPING SAUCE:
Mix together all the ingredients in a small bowl. Marinate 15 minutes before serving.

Why Annette rolls

Once assembled, these spring rolls look like layers of delicate, silky lingerie. They're a perfect finger food, and I feel sexy when I eat them. The chile dipping sauce tingles and tantalizes the tongue with stinging heat.

honey-almond
home cured snapper

Brillat-Savarin, the most celebrated of culinary philosophers, touted fish as containing, "the most combustible elements in nature," and that a diet based on fish is the "most heating."

I've been curing fish for dinner guests for years to showers of praise. I actually question my own logic in giving away the secret here to my signature dish's nearly idiot-proof simplicity. It's really the reactions of my dinner guests, which very much reflect the suggestions of Brillat-Savarin, that made me decide to divulge my precious secret.

Although the combination of honey and almonds was a classic among the lusty ancient Greeks, this aphrodisiac combination is an experiment all my own. It evolved from an experiment to try to compound the sensuality of cured fish with the nutrients of almonds and the viscosity of honey.

While most cured fish is rinsed before serving, I prefer to leave the fish in this recipe unwashed in a celebration of textures—the crunch of coarsely chopped almonds against the smooth flesh.

preparation

Rinse fish and pat dry. Lay raw flesh flat in a shallow baking dish on a fresh sheet of plastic wrap large enough to thoroughly double-wrap the fish. Gently rub salt into both sides of flesh. Drench with honey and rum, then top with the nuts. Wrap flesh tightly in the plastic top with a plate or smaller baking dish so that the flesh is pinned to the bottom dish. Weight the plate with soup cans or anything heavy enough to add pressure.

After refrigerating for 24 hours, flip fish and continue to weight for an additional 24 hours. Cured flesh is ready to serve after 48 hours but can continue to cure for an additional two days.

To serve, thinly slice with your sharpest knife, leaving a generous topping of almonds. Serve with crostini or crackers, minced onions, thinly shaved cucumber, and softened cream cheese.

1/2 lb fresh snapper*
2 1/2 T honey
1 1/2 T coarse salt
1 T light rum
2 T lightly salted,
    roasted almonds,
    coarsely crushed

*This recipe relies on high-quality, super-fresh fish. It works well with nearly every white-fleshed fish from snapper to sea bass to mahimahi.

starters

something fishy, my sweet

A plate of cured fish is one dish I know will always disappear in a mixed crowd. I've even caught guests trailing a finger through the damp smear of salt and sweetness left on the empty plate and then positively licking it clean. After my guests have nibbled this sensual snack, I've noticed that eyes seem to turn overly bright as though lit by a Hollywood film crew, lips turn up more than usual, and I've secretly observed more than one couple disappearing soon after the appetizer.

zucchini stuffed with warm lobster

by Nitzi Rabin, star chef, restaurateur and provocateur from Chillingsworth restaurant in Brewster, MA

Lobster is one of the most sensuous foods in a chef's goodie bag. Long linked with amorous pursuits, the lobster has been connected with every legendary lothario since Casanova. In more modern times, its indelible mark as a catalyst for passion has been captured on film in climactic moments in works from *Flashdance* to the unforgettable *Tom Jones*. Here it is unsheathed from its complicated shell for even easier access and then infused with vanilla's scent of passion.

preparation

Preheat oven to 300 degrees.

Section zucchini into 4 even, hollowed-out logs. (Zucchini can be hollowed out with the tip of a vegetable peeler.) Roast the zucchini logs on the middle oven rack until just tender to the touch, about 15–20 minutes. Set your logs aside to cool.

In a medium saucepan gently heat the cream, adding chopped leek along with the garlic. Cook slowly for 10–15 minutes, just long enough to flavor the cream. Strain out leek and garlic, then season the cream with salt and pepper. Add the split vanilla bean to your warm, fragrant cream and simmer to infuse the vanilla flavor to your liking. Remove the bean and set it aside. Stir in the saffron and reduce cream over medium heat to a sauce consistency, watching carefully to prevent it from boiling over. Adjust seasoning. (Cream sauce can be prepared ahead.)

Add celery and jicama to sauce and cook for 1 or 2 minutes, and then add the lobster. Gently warm through.

Cover baking dish of zucchini with aluminum foil and return to the oven to reheat, about 4–5 minutes.

To serve, place 2 tender zucchini in the cen-

3/4 lb cooked lobster meat, cut in a 1/2 inch dice
1 large zucchini
1 leek, green tops discarded
1/8 t garlic, minced
2 T jicama, finely diced
2 T peeled and deveined celery, finely diced
1/2 vanilla bean, split lengthwise
1 t powdered saffron, (or saffron threads toasted and pulverized)
1 T chervil, chopped
1 1/2 T ripe roma tomato, seeded and minced
2 c heavy cream
sea salt and white pepper to taste
fresh chervil for garnish

ter of each of 2 plates. Stuff the hot logs with the creamy lobster mixture, allowing some to overflow. Spoon additional cream into zucchini and drizzle more onto the plate. Sprinkle chopped chervil and minced tomato over your warm lobster cream and garnish with chervil sprigs.

the chef shares confessions from the dining table

Each night after the dinner service at my restaurant, Chillingsworth, I have a tradition of visiting with the patrons in the dining room. I have served this appetizer on numerous occasions to what I would call a "rapturous" reception.

I've found that most guests like to share with me how they're feeling from this cream-smothered dining drug. Those are the times when I count on my pastry staff to rush the dessert course, if you know what I mean.

peach lover's summer gazpacho

Fruit soup, popular in Scandinavia but relatively uncommon in North America, is a flavor that sends shock waves from the tongue to the brain. Because we're not used to seeing something that looks like soup but tastes sweet, the first sip always jolts the senses and immediately brings the palate and mind to a heightened state of awareness.

preparation

In a blender, combine the peaches, honeydew, orange juice, 1 T basil and a couple pinches of salt. Blend to a smooth cream.

Pour cold soup into wine glasses and garnish with cheese and remaining basil.

Serve cold or at room temperature.

2 c peaches, peeled and diced
1 c honeydew, diced
1/2 c orange juice
1 T fresh basil, coarsely chopped
salt to taste
1 T crumbled chevre (optional)
1 T fresh basil, minced

While I find editing a book on aphrodisiacs easy, I must admit that cooking them is not one of my primary strengths. But I was drawn to the simplicity and straightforwardness of this recipe. After tasting the smooth and surprising chilly sensory pleasure of this soup, I had to call my newlywed sister to share the soup's secret. (The peach delight worked equally well for her.)

honey carrot soup

by Chef Daisie Armstrong, Cordon Bleu grad and culinary flirt

Daisie originally created this soup as a recipe for my newsletter, *Aphrodisiac of the Month.* We were looking for a taste that elicited both dimensions of comfort and surprise. Daisie and I both love this nectar-laced tongue warmer for its velvety texture, but what is probably most appealing is the way the honey teases out the natural sweetness of the carrots.

preparation

Heat the olive oil in a medium sauce pot. Add the onion and a pinch of salt. Cook until onions turn translucent. Add the carrots, garlic and chicken broth and bring to a boil. Cook until carrots are tender.

Transfer the solids to a blender and add enough chicken broth to just cover the solids. Blend until smooth. Add more chicken broth to adjust thickness to your preference.

Return soup to another pot (or same one if you used all the broth) and bring to a boil. Bring to a simmer and add the milk and honey. Do not boil after this point.

Cook until heated through and add the nutmeg. Adjust seasoning with salt and pepper if needed. Top with chives before serving.

Note: To make a vegetarian version, swap vegetable stock for chicken stock and use soymilk in place of the dairy.

1 lb carrots, peeled and sliced
2 16 oz cans reduced sodium chicken broth
1 medium yellow onion, chopped
1 garlic clove, minced
1 T olive oil
1 c low fat milk
1/4 c honey
1/4 t ground nutmeg
2 T chives, chopped for garnish
salt and pepper to taste

the chef spills

Daisie hasn't tried it out as a segue to seduction yet, but that's because she's still searching for an adventurous spirit to share her love of sweet carrots.

main courses

love linguine with almond pesto
almond

saffron-basil matzo ball soup
saffron

rosemary potato salad
with fat sausages
rosemary

soft poached eggs on
saffron dressed salad
saffron

green tea poached salmon
with sensual salsa
mango

vanilla-scented sea bass
with a red hot rub
vanilla

lamb burgers with my sweet
peach chutney
peach

moist mango meatloaf
mango

rosemary skewered chicken on
a bed of roasted roots
rosemary

hard tacos with hot guacamole
chile

fire grilled chops with
horseradish-mint sauce
mint

love linguine with almond pesto

Pesto is an ancient sauce of lusty, Italian origins that can be traced back as far as 17th century Genoa. Traditionalists believe pesto can be made only by hand-crushing the ingredients with a mortar and pestle. However, this machine-blended method frees hands for other indoor sports.

preparation

2 T toasted almonds
1 large clove garlic, sliced
3 c fresh basil
2 T parmesan cheese (2 oz)
2 T lemon juice
3 T olive oil
salt to taste
1 lb dried linguine pasta

In a blender or food processor, pulse almonds. Add garlic, basil, cheese, and lemon juice, processing to a pulp. Add oil slowly in a fine stream and blend until creamy.

Prepare linguine according to instructions. Top with pesto and toss to thoroughly coat.

For a more substantial meal, you can enhance your pasta with crumbled goat cheese, shredded roasted chicken, or steamed clams.

it's so easy being green

Although they are considered aphrodisiacs, pine nuts, the traditional main ingredient in pesto, just don't do it for me. So here I trade them for less bitter and slightly crunchier almonds, which lend both their flavor and texture to this sexy sauce.

saffron-basil
matzo ball soup

This version plays with the original flavor of matzo, introducing aromatic basil (also an aphrodisiac) to the otherwise nondescript dough. A base of saffron brings a compelling richness and a vibrant goldenrod color to the broth.

preparation

FOR THE SAFFRON CHICKEN BROTH:

Bring all ingredients to a boil in a large stockpot. Turn temperature to low and simmer for 30 minutes or until chicken meat is falling off bones.

Remove chicken from the amber liquid and strain stock into another large pot. Once chicken cools, pull the meat from the bones, mince, and reserve for the soup. (Stock can be made up to two days in advance and stored in the refrigerator.)

FOR THE BASIL MATZO BALLS:

Whisk eggs, salt, and oil in a medium bowl. Blend in the matzo meal, then the basil. Cover and chill in the fridge until firm, at least 1 hour.

Bring large pot of generously salted water to a boil. Using moist hands, coax matzo mixture into 8 balls, using about 2 T of the dough for each. Gently drop matzo balls into boiling water. Immediately reduce heat to low, cover pot, and

FOR THE SAFFRON CHICKEN BROTH:
2 12 oz cans low sodium chicken broth
1/2 t saffron threads
1 lb chicken wings and/or thighs*

*For a shortcut, use 1 lb boneless, precooked, roasted chicken. It will save time, but the soup will lose the intensity of flavor that is drawn from the bones.

main courses

FOR THE BASIL MATZO
BALLS:
2 large eggs
1 t salt
2 T vegetable oil
1/2 c matzo meal
1/2 c fresh basil,
    chopped

simmer until balls are tender, about 35 minutes. Remove immediately from boiling water and save 1/2 c cooking water. (Matzo balls can be made up to 24 hours in advance, dried on paper towels, and stored covered in the refrigerator.)

TO MAKE THE SOUP:

Heat stock and chicken in a large pot. Once the soup is simmering, add cooked matzo balls and 1/2 c cooking water and simmer to heat through, about 10 minutes. Ladle 2 balls into each bowl and submerge with the simmering, golden stock.

the tale of a man who can boil water but would never cook soup

You might be wondering what's so sexy about a bowl of chicken soup.

I know a man who absolutely refuses to cook but can heat a mean bowl of soup. As a matter of fact, I think he eats soup five or more times a week, even in summer. Who better to test the recipe than this connoisseur of soup?

I am not one to kiss and tell, but I will share with you this much—when I ladled the basil-sweet broth into a bowl, I unleashed in my soup connoisseur an altogether unexpected yet undeniably scrumptious reaction.

main courses

rosemary potato salad with fat sausages

by Chef Daisie Armstrong

Like little blank canvases, potatoes are wonderful for soaking up the flavors of other ingredients. They are perfect for combining with the sharp herbal taste of rosemary and the salt and fat of smoky sausage. From the moment Daisie first introduced to me this recipe, I was sold on both its perfect harmony of flavors and the sixth-grade humor of its name.

preparation

With a vigorous stroke, whisk vinegar, mustard, rosemary, garlic, and allspice in a small bowl. Gradually whisk in the olive oil. Season to taste with salt and pepper. Set dressing aside.

Bring a large pot of salted water to a boil. Drop whole, unpeeled potatoes in boiling water and bring back to a boil. Cook potatoes until they feel tender when pierced by a fork. This should take approximately 15 min. Drain and let stand about 10 minutes. Cut the potatoes, skin still on, into 1/4 inch rounds. Your potatoes may naturally split or crumble. This only adds to the salad's rustic vibe.

1 1/2 T white wine vinegar
1 T Dijon mustard
2 t fresh rosemary, finely minced
2 cloves garlic
1/4 t ground allspice
3 T olive oil
salt & pepper to taste
6 small red potatoes
1 leek, halved length-wise, rinsed, and finely chopped
1/2 lb fully cooked smoked sausage, cut into 1/4 inch rounds
1 oz Roquefort cheese, crumbled
fresh rosemary sprigs for garnish

In a large bowl, dress potatoes in half of the dressing. Gently toss the leek and sausage into the mix and coat with remaining dressing. Stir in the cheese and adjust salt to taste. Garnish with fresh rosemary sprigs and serve with passion.

Daisie's Desire

Before she ever knew of rosemary's romantic properties, Daisie spiced up her lust life with this potato salad—and not just because she can't resist fat sausages. She recommends taking a bite with closed eyes to fully savor the sensation of the vinegar and Dijon tingling the tongue.

soft-poached egg
on a saffron dressed salad

by Master Chef James Corwell,
wine country Casanova

This is a variation on a classic French bistro salad but one that pushes Chef Corwell's buttons in ways far beyond those of bistro dining. Here, Corwell excites the tongue by lacing the basic oil and vinegar dressing with more robust flavor than the original. The result is a very rewarding pairing with the richness of a creamy, soft-poached egg.

preparation

In a small sauté pan, heat the olive oil and the bacon over medium low heat; turn periodically until bacon is very crisp. Remove bacon to paper towels and blot; hold in a warm oven. Do not discard the oil in the pan.

Add garlic to the bacon cooking oil and toss

1/4 c olive oil

4 slices bacon, cut into
thin strips

1/4 c garlic, sliced thin

1 firm, red tomato,
grated on a box
grater

1 t paprika

1/2 t saffron, crushed

1/4 c sherry vinegar

1 lemon

4 poached eggs, soft

1 c toasted croutons

4 c dandelion greens,
trimmed to fork-
sized pieces*

4 Belgium endives,
julienne

*If you can't find dande-
lion greens, substitute
arugula, an equally bit-
ter, but somewhat more
peppery green.

constantly until golden brown. Immediately add tomato, paprika, and saffron; stir and fry until tomato pulp becomes thick, about 3-4 minutes.

Remove tomato mixture from the heat and add vinegar and a squeeze of fresh lemon, just enough to balance the vinaigrette's flavor. Add salt and pepper to taste.

Warm poached eggs and toss croutons, dandelion, endive, and reserved bacon in a light amount of vinaigrette. Taste and adjust salad seasoning with additional salt, pepper, lemon or vinegar. Arrange greens on two serving plates.

Place warm eggs over each salad; season egg to your heart's desire with some salt and pepper and additional vinaigrette before serving.

a quote from the master

In many ways your taste in food can be used to describe your taste in partners. To me, saffron, being a rarer spice, represents some of the most beautiful women that I have known. This exotic flower is slow, so slow to release its flavor, yet powerful in its ability to stain any dish with its unmatched, golden color. When used wisely it becomes that secret ingredient that creates a startlingly unique dish. Although its flavor hints more at metallic than sweet, I would describe it as the taste of a kiss to your lover's body—it cannot be overestimated.

green tea-poached salmon with sensual salsa

Salmon, green tea, ginger, basil, and of course, mango—all touted among the world's most potent aphrodisiacs—transform this simple dish into a veritable Viagra salad.

preparation

Gently tie basil, thyme, and cilantro stems with white cotton string. (In chef speak, you've created a bouquet garni.)

In a sauté pan, bring bouquet garni, lemon juice, lemon zest, fresh ginger, and tea to a stimulating simmer. Add the salmon filets and poach for 7 minutes or until opaque. Remove pan from heat and let salmon cool down in poaching liquid.

FOR THE SALSA:

Transfer all ingredients to a bowl. Hand-toss the fleshy fruit and season with salt to taste (finger-licking required).

Rest each cool, pink filet on a bed of baby greens. Lubricate with two tablespoons of sensual summer salsa. Enjoy.

FOR THE SALMON:
3 sprigs fresh basil
3 sprigs fresh thyme
3 sprigs fresh cilantro
1 medium lemon, juice and zest
2 T fresh ginger root, coarsely chopped
2 c strong green tea, brewed
2 4 oz salmon filets
1 c baby greens

FOR THE SALSA:
1/2 mango, peeled and chopped
1 ripe apricot, pitted and chopped
1 scallion, thinly sliced
1 T fresh cilantro, chopped
1 t lemon zest
1 T lemon juice
1 T crystallized ginger, minced
salt to taste

dancing the salsa

In reality, no food is going to inspire a command performance with the conviction of Viagra, but if you ask me, this dish at once satisfies hunger and provokes a more primal appetite. I love the contrasting textures—the slippery flesh of poached fish against the crunch of the salsa. But it's that last little detail that gets me every time— the tease of sweet, hot ginger tossed on my fruit.

vanilla-scented sea bass with a red hot rub

by Chef Neil Wigglesworth, culinary king and chief of romance for Twin Farms, Barnard Vermont

Most recipes in this book are designed for working magic once they tickle the taste buds. But the sensual experience of this aromatic dish begins in the kitchen. Keep your lover close at hand as you simmer the vanilla-scented sauce, for the aroma alone of a fine vanilla bean is a known sexual stimulant.

preparation

Season fish with salt and pepper. Turn skin side up, and using a sharp knife, score the skin lengthwise, about 5 times per piece. With firm pressure, massage the chile powder into the scores. Reserve covered in the refrigerator.

In a sauce pot, bring fish stock to a simmer then reduce heat. Scrape vanilla from pod into your simmering sauce; add the vanilla extract and the two halves of your vanilla pod. Simmer until liquid is reduced by half. Allow your sauce to cool, and then remove vanilla bean pod and strain through a fine strainer.

Preheat oven to 400 degrees.

In a sauté pan heat oil, thoroughly coating bottom of pan. Over medium heat add fish, skin side down, and cook for 4–5 minutes until skin is a delicious caramel color. Flip the fillets and sear on flesh side to lock in the juices, about 1 minute.

Remove from pan and transfer to oven to finish cooking the fish's firm flesh for 4–5 minutes.

To finish, reheat the vanilla-scented stock and slowly add cream. Do not allow your sauce to boil once you've added your cream. Using a hand-held mixer (or wire whisk), add in the butter. Sauce will begin to foam. Serve sauce warm and foamy over your baked fish fillets. Garnish with fresh tarragon.

2 4 oz sea bass filets, skin on
salt & pepper
1 T ancho chile powder
3 c fish stock
1 whole vanilla bean, split
1/2 T vanilla extract
1 1/2 T canola oil
1/2 c heavy cream
3 T salted butter
2 sprigs fresh tarragon

main courses

the chef's suggestions for serving sensuality

I serve this fish over crushed parsnips, a mildly flavored root vegetable in the turnip family. The aroma of the vanilla, the sweetness of the parsnips, and the bite of the smoky chile combined with the fresh sea flavor of the bass get my heart racing every time. Or maybe I'm confusing it with the cholesterol effects from the butter and cream! Whatever the catalyst, my advice in the kitchen—and in any other room—is to keep it simple and keep it hot.

lamb burgers with my sweet peach chutney

The secret to these burgers is the special sauce spiked with cranberries. Noted among nature's aphrodisiacs, the cranberries pull a tartness into the chutney that makes the taste buds dance. Here they are mingled with the soft flesh of peaches as a replacement for the raisins of more traditional chutneys. They bring a similar element of texture without raisins' slightly prune-like sweetness.

main courses

preparation

Mix meat with remaining ingredients until the mixture is good and spicy. Shape into two thick patties. Set aside.

In a small food processor, combine shallot, ginger and garlic. Pulse until finely chopped.

Heat olive oil in a large sauté pan over medium heat. In the sizzling oil, toss shallot mixture until tender and fragrant, about 2 minutes.

Add remaining ingredients and bring chutney to a boil. Cover and reduce heat to low. Continue cooking 20 minutes. Adjust seasoning with salt, if needed. Then let your sweet chutney cool to room temperature.

(Chutney can be made 1 to 2 days in advance and refrigerated. Warm to room temperature before serving.)

TO ASSEMBLE:

Grill burgers over medium-high heat to desired doneness.

Warm pitas slightly in oven or microwave.

Split each pita and fill your pockets with lettuce, onions and your tangy chutney. Slice the burgers in half and stuff meat into warm pitas.

FOR THE BURGERS:
1/2 lb ground lamb
1/4 t chile powder
1/4 t ground cumin
pinch allspice
salt to taste

FOR THE CHUTNEY:
1 large shallot, cut in
    half
1 T fresh ginger, peeled
1 clove garlic, peeled
1 T extra virgin olive oil
1 T lemon zest
1/3 c fresh lemon juice
1/2 t chile powder
1 t red wine vinegar
2 T light brown sugar
2 medium peaches,
    peeled and cut into
    1/2-inch chunks
1 c fresh cranberries
1/2 t salt

TO ASSEMBLE:
1 c baby lettuce
sweet Maui or Vidalia
    onion, thinly sliced
2 pita bread rounds

main courses

my sweet spot

I like to be experimental in my aphrodisiac experiences. I've tried the chutney on salmon burgers, buffalo meat, and even chicken salad. But it is definitely in the mingling with the slightly gamey taste of lamb that this sweet, tart sauce most powerfully arouses my senses.

moist mango meatloaf

2 lbs ground beef or turkey
2 t salt
1 t ground black pepper
2 t curry powder
1 t chile powder
1 clove garlic, finely minced
2 eggs
1 yellow onion, finely chopped
1/4 c orange juice
1 medium mango, peeled & diced

Conventional wisdom says that sexy foods are light on the stomach. So how can meatloaf fit the model? By adding sweet, succulent fruit and cutting down the fat, this meaty slice of Americana shows you can lust for meat and eat it, too.

preparation

Preheat oven to 350.

In a large bowl, mix all ingredients together thoroughly. Mold into a loaf pan, cover with plastic wrap, and chill for 1 hour. Remove plastic wrap and bake for 1 hour or until probe thermometer (a.k.a., meat thermometer) reads 160 degrees when slowly inserted into the loaf's thick center. Remove from oven and let rest for 5–10 minutes to finish cooking.

my relationship with meat

I'm not much for meatloaf. So to answer the cravings of the meat lovers in my life, I invented this version of the American classic with a nod to my preference for exotic spice. The mango makes it juicy, not to mention oh-so-sweet. Curry compounds the complexity of flavors without evolving the dish into something too tropical. And of course, the main ingredient remains true to the original: an abundance of moist meat.

rosemary skewered chicken on a bed of roasted roots

by Annette Tomei, private chef and woman who wines

Fresh rosemary adds more than edgy flavor, it also makes a perfect skewer.

preparation

Wash and dry the rosemary skewers. Leaving approximately two inches of leaves tickling the top

main courses

6 branches of fresh rosemary, approximately 6 inches in length

12 oz boneless skinless chicken breast cut into 1 in cubes

juice and zest of one lemon

1 t Dijon mustard

1/4 c of olive oil

1/2 t sea salt

1/2 t freshly ground black pepper

2 T fresh rosemary leaves (reserved from stripped skewers)

of each branch, remove remaining leaves and reserve 2 tablespoons. Trim and clean up the stems to use as skewers. This can be done up to two days in advance. (Store the reserved leaves in a zip top bag and the branches wrapped in damp paper towels in the refrigerator until you're ready for action.)

Heat a grill or stovetop grill pan to high. (You can also oven bake the chicken although you will lose that hint of char. If baking, preheat the oven to 350 degrees.)

Chop the reserved rosemary leaves and place in a medium mixing bowl with the lemon zest, juice, Dijon mustard, olive oil, salt and pepper. Whisk with a brisk motion.

Toss in the chicken pieces. Cover and allow the chicken to marinate in the fridge for 30 minutes, or if you get preoccupied, you can leave it for up to one hour.

Divvy up the chicken cubes evenly among the rosemary skewers and skewer all your meat. If grilling, lightly brush the grill grates with oil. If baking, wrap the leaf ends of the skewers in aluminum foil, line a baking sheet with foil, and brush it lightly with oil.

To grill, place the skewers with the leaf ends away from the heat. Grill for approximately 5 minutes on each of four sides or until firm and evenly cooked. If baking, cook for approximately 10 minutes, flip the skewers, and bake for an additional 10 minutes or until the chicken is cooked through. When ready, your meat should be nice and firm.

Serve hot or at room temperature (within 2 hours of cooking) over roasted root vegetables.

Preheat the grill to high or the oven to 400 degrees.

FOR THE ROASTED ROOTS:

Throw all the ingredients in a large bowl and toss well with your fingers to coat evenly.

To cook on the grill, make a double-layered pouch from heavy-duty foil. Place the vegetables in the center of the foil and wrap, folding edges carefully to prevent your juice from leaking. Transfer the pouch to the grill on a baking sheet. Cook for approximately one hour. Be careful of steam and sweet baking juices when you open your hot package.

If you prefer baking in the oven, prepare a 13x9x2 baking pan with non-stick spray. Add the vegetables. Cover with foil. Roast in a 400 degree oven for approximately 45 minutes or until fork tender.

Season with salt and pepper to taste before serving.

Makes enough for leftovers.

FOR THE ROASTED ROOTS:

1/2 c butternut squash, peeled and diced

1/4 c sweet potato or yam, peeled and diced

1 small bulb of fennel, cleaned and sliced

4 cipollini onions, peeled and halved

1 medium red beet (or 4 baby beets), peeled and diced

1 fresh pear, cored and diced

1 T fresh rosemary leaves, chopped

1 t dried lavender, chopped

1 t salt

1/2 t fresh ground pepper

2 T olive oil

juice and zest of one medium orange

1 1/2 T honey

salt and pepper

main courses

Comfort food can be the ultimate provocateur. (And I have firsthand knowledge on this one.) The richness of the roots, the perfume of the rosemary and lavender, and the sweetness of the vegetables and honey, combine to encourage snuggles and warm kisses for dessert.

hard tacos with hot guacamole

Guacamole is a sexy food. Even the name smacks of something naughty. But more enticing than its name is its main ingredient, avocados.

The ancient Aztecs were the first to dub avocados as aphrodisiacs. They even named the fruit after the word for testicle. In ancient times, this sensual, soft-fleshed fruit was reserved for royalty, as a gourmet treat of great power. Even in the United States, the fruit is ripe with aphrodisiac lore. A nationwide advertising campaign in the 1920s claimed that the denial of avocados could have an aphrodisiac effect, leaving them wanting more of what they couldn't have. In the advertising world, this reverse campaign was considered a tremendous success.

Here, hot guac is paired with tacos, the South of the Border sandwich. A balancing act of hard and creamy textures, chile spice, salt and fat, these tacos capture every flavor craving.

preparation

Toss tomato, jalapeno, green onion and 1/2 tablespoon of lime juice in a small bowl. Reserve.

Peel your avocado. In a small bowl, mash the moist flesh with a fork. Stir in cilantro, lemon juice, milk, chile and salt to taste. Save for later.

Heat oil in a large skillet over medium high heat. Heat your meat for 5 minutes or until browned. Season well and stir to break up the lumps. Drain off any extra oil and remove meat from pan, reserving for later. Return pan to heat and cook the onion until translucent. Add the garlic, chipotles with sauce, cinnamon, and hot meat. Bring to a simmer and cook for 5 minutes. Serve steaming in taco shells with tomatoes, cilantro, guacamole and cheese. Stuffs 6–8 shells.

FOR THE GUACAMOLE:
1 ripe avocado
1 T fresh cilantro, finely chopped
1 T lemon juice
1 t milk
1/2 t chile powder
coarse salt to taste

1 t canola oil
1 medium brown onion, minced
1 clove garlic, minced
1/2 can chipotle chiles in adobo sauce, chopped
1 t cinnamon
salt and pepper to taste
1 lb ground beef or turkey
1 1/2 T fresh lime juice
1/4 c fresh cilantro, chopped
3 T white cheddar cheese, shredded
1 medium tomato, diced
1/2 jalapeno pepper, seeded and finely minced (optional)
1 green onion, diced

main courses

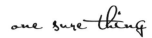

one sure thing

I've always been attracted to one-dish meals. Any recipe that promises next to no cleanup is an aphrodisiac in my mind. Add to that my love for the locker room humor of anything stuffed with hot meat and you've pretty much hit a home run. Slather with guacamole and served with a potent shot of tequila and you've got a "sure thing."

fire grilled chops with horseradish-mint sauce

Adding horseradish, an ancient Greek remedy for low libido, to mint sauce really bumps up the aphrodisiac factor for this recipe. For lovers who like it spicy, add a smidge of extra horseradish for a naughty little kick. Not sure how much is just enough? Close your eyes and let your tongue be your guide.

Although I use mini lamb chops as the meat, the method works with everything from pork to turkey tenderloin.

preparation

In a small bowl, combine first three ingredients. Salt to taste. (Can be prepared 1 day ahead. Cover and refrigerate.)

Preheat your grill to medium. (Chops are petite, so be careful not to burn.) Combine mustard and garlic and massage into both sides of your chops. Season the meat with salt and pepper. Grill lamb to desired doneness.

Serve with your creamy sauce on the side. Baby chops should be eaten with fingers. Forking the lamb is frowned upon.

Note: If there is any sauce left over, save it. This incredibly versatile cream is great for serving as a dressing for grilled chicken salad, as a veggie dip, or simply as a mint-tinged massage cream.

1/2 c sour cream
2 t prepared horseradish
1 T chopped fresh mint
1 T Dijon mustard
1 large garlic clove, minced
3/4 lb thin-cut baby lamb chops*
salt and pepper

*You may have to pre-order thinly cut chops from your butcher, as they are generally considered a specialty item.

carnivore confessions

Grilled meat isn't usually my thing, and I know it's cliché to say that a creamy white sauce makes all the difference. But I love this recipe's tangy sauce so much I could scoop it by the spoonful. In my opinion, it tastes best licked from the warm fingers of my favorite dinner companion.

sauces & libations

dipping green goddess
rosemary

chile rub
chile

mint butter
mint

sweet and hot apricot sauce
honey

not wholly mole
chocolate

hard sauce
vanilla

a word on wine

a paragraph on port

more potent elixirs

magic mint syrup
mint

white peach Bellini
peach

saffron fleurtation
saffron

a very sexy cocktail
fig

honey drop
honey

bloody maria
chile

ginger mojito
ginger

dipping green goddess

Although it can be hard to make a bowl of vegetables seem sexy, green goddess adds a certain finesse. I first fell for a version of the goddess made by Chef Mark Peel of Los Angeles' restaurant, Campanile. Peel served green goddess-dressed greens with seared, fresh tuna. The base of the dish may have been little more than a bowl of grass, but combined with the fatty, raw tuna flesh and the tinge of creamy dressing, the dish gave new meaning to the journalistic phrase "food porn."

My version simplifies the steps to making the tangy dip and switches it up as a finger food. Served with slender carrot and asparagus spears, it brings very suggestive pleasure to getting that food pyramid's daily minimum.

1/2 c mayo
2 T chives, chopped
2 T parsley, chopped
1 1/2 t fresh rosemary, finely minced
1 T lemon juice
1/2 t Worcestershire sauce
1/4 t dry mustard
1/4 t garlic, finely chopped
1 t fresh tarragon, minced

preparation

Add all ingredients to blender and pulse to a smooth, herb-green cream.

Serve as a cool dip for your favorite fresh, young vegetables, such as blanched zucchini and asparagus, carrot spears and cucumber wedges.

chile rub

by Stephan Juliusburger, former road chef to the
Grateful Dead

Around the time I met him, Stephan Julius-burger, former road chef for the Grateful Dead, traded in his chef whites for the culinary classroom, surrounded by the pink sand of Bermuda. With more leisure time on his hands, he keeps busy concocting flavor-spiked labors of love like this one. But to take the grunt out of the work, he advises sharing this task with a partner in love: "We peel, toast, and grind together, allowing the spices to seep under the skin of our fingers as the pungent smells intoxicate us. Then we rub the finished product into the raw meat…. In short, making this rub usually puts an end to the dinner preparations. It's the main reason we let the food rest for two hours before cooking—we need the time.

While writing this recipe for me, Stephan added this instructional love note, "As with any recipe, cher Amy, the devil (or in this case cherub) is in the details. In order for this rub to result in aphrodisiacal bliss, some work is involved in advance. This is why I have given quantities for a larger amount. This rub can be stored either frozen, in a truly airtight container, or, for best results, in vacuum bags, for up to 3 months without impacting its freshness (or its effect on the diner)."

sauces & libations

1/4 c whole white pepper
1/4 c dried whole ancho chile
1 T dried whole chipotle
1/4 c olive oil
1/4 c garlic, sliced in 1/8 inch slices
1/4 c salt
1/4 c cayenne
1/4 c ground cumin
1/4 c ground coriander
1/4 c paprika

Take whole peppercorns and grind them with a mortar and pestle. (Do not use pre-ground pepper. It usually will have been ground years ago and will taste harsh and acrid.)

Take dried chiles, slice in half, and remove the stems and seeds. Dry toast them in a skillet and then grind.

Heat 1/4 c olive oil (not extra virgin) in a skillet. When oil is hot, add garlic, turning slices with a wooden spatula until they are light gold on both sides. (Over browning will turn the garlic bitter.) Remove from oil and drain on paper towel. Once chips are dry and crisp, grind with mortar and pestle.

You can save the garlic-infused oil in an airtight jar for cooking your next stir-fry.

Combine prepared chiles and garlic with remaining spices. Apply enough rub to cover liberally and evenly to all sides of your choice of meat or fish. Make sure that you rub the mix into your flesh. Place on a rack over a sheet pan and let sit in the refrigerator for 2 hours before cooking.

Grill the meat or fish. If possible, add a few dampened mesquite flakes to the fire just before cooking—heavenly!

The male perspective— Stephan speaks out

Although I may have used food to seduce as a youngster, one has to be careful with spices, as they can prove very painful to the eyes and other...sensitive areas...if applied directly. The eating of spiced food is very erotic, though. It inflames the taste buds and even more so the sense of smell, which I believe can lead to excited pheromones, and we all know where that leads.

I have never reprised the jalapeno and blindfold à la *9-1/2 Weeks*, but the old adage of the way to a man's (woman's) heart does definitely apply in the real world. There's a reason why clichés become so.

sauces & libations

mint butter

Much of mint's aphrodisiac potency is in its scent. (The reason so many aromatherapy oils and breath mints employ its fresh fragrance.) And this simple recipe is perfect for showcasing the herb's sexy smell.

preparation

1/2 c butter, warmed to room temperature
1 T mint, finely minced

Put mint and butter into a small bowl and cream together. Then place in an airtight dish and refrigerate. To keep for a longer time, cool slightly in the refrigerator, then form the mint butter into a sausage-shaped roll. Wrap tightly in plastic and store in the freezer for up to two weeks. To use, slice off wedges of the frozen butter as needed.

smear campaign

Spread the butter on lemon muffins, brush it on pineapple and grill the fruit, top roast lamb or poached lobster with the alluring compound and allow the fragrance to release both into the sauce and into the air. Although these are my favorite uses for this divine lubricant, its uses need not be limited by anything more than your imagination.

sauces & libations

sweet and hot
apricot sauce

*by Chef Ivy Haaks, creator of Whole Haute
organic delivery in Los Angeles*

When eaten fresh, apricots—aphrodisiacs in their own right—can be teasingly tangy, and more importantly, they have the kind of juice that dribbles down your palm and along the soft flesh inside your arm —ripe for the licking!

But when apricots are dried, the fruit's concentrated sugars take on an entirely new richness. I like things sweet, and I love Ivy's recipe because the shot of fruit sugar is compounded by the sweet viscosity of golden honey.

preparation

Place the dried apricots into a bowl and cover with boiling water. Soak in the hot bath for 1/2 hour.

Drain off the liquid from the apricots and reserve.

Place the apricots into a food processor and add in the cinnamon, honey, dried chile (for less heat omit the seeds and white interior veins), lemon juice and work into a puree. While the food processor is on, add in slowly up to a cup of the apricot soaking liquid to make a smooth

1 cup dried apricots
1/2 t cinnamon
2 T honey
1 dried red chile with
    seeds
juice of 1 lemon
pinch of salt and black
    pepper

sauces & libations

sauce consistency. To finish, season with a pinch of salt and black pepper.

Makes about 1 1/2 c dipping sauce.

*the word from
a sweet pro*

I created this recipe to combine flavor-rich and nutrient-dense dried apricots with chile and honey, nature's perfect stimulants. I rely on it when I need a last minute flavor booster; it can be prepared in a pinch and stored in the refrigerator to be called upon for just the right occasion.

The beauty of this sauce is its versatility (and its recipe for romantic success). I like to grill some chicken kabobs and use the sauce for dipping—as in with my fingers. Lamb is equally suited for this spicy-sweet sauce, as is fresh fruit. Place a bowl of the sauce in the center of a freshly prepared fruit plate, sprinkle with mint, and let your fingers do the walking.

sauces & libations

not wholly mole

The word mole comes from the Aztec word "molli," which loosely translates to stew or sauce. The Aztecs were among the first to embrace chocolate as an aphrodisiac, and this sauce is one of the finest concoctions ever invented to incorporate chocolate into savory dishes.

Traditional mole is not for the timid cook. Mole normally takes intense preparation, a time commitment unrealistic in most modern American homes.

I've distilled the steps, and while totally inauthentic, the sauce does capture mole's lusty flavors. To use not wholly mole in the traditional fashion, slow-cook turkey or chicken by simmering it in the thick, cocoa-scented sauce.

preparation

In a large heavy skillet, sauté the onions in the oil over moderately high heat and stir until they turn golden brown. Stir coriander powder into the onions. Add the chile powder, sugar, cinnamon, allspice and cloves. Cook the mixture over medium heat, stirring for 1 minute. Slowly pour in 1 cup of broth and tomatoes and add cocoa powder, peanut butter, garlic and salt to taste. Let your sauce simmer, uncovered, stirring occasionally for 20 minutes. Sauce should be the

1 c chopped onion
1 T vegetable oil
1/2 t coriander powder
1 1/2 T chile powder
1 t sugar
1 t cinnamon
1/4 t allspice
1/4 t ground cloves
1–1 1/2 c chicken broth
1 lb can tomatoes, drained and chopped
2 T unsweetened cocoa powder
1 T natural almond or peanut butter
1 clove of garlic, minced
salt to taste

sauces & libations

consistency of heavy cream. If your sauce gets too thick, thin it slightly by adding chicken broth.

For a creamy sauce, pulse in blender until smooth.

Simmer chunks of chicken meat or beef in sauce or serve over baked fish, sautéed vegetables or tofu.

mole mama

I have a friend whose Mexican parents, raised her on mole. And although the thick, chocolaty sauce left an indelible impression on her tongue, my friend shunned the hours of intense labor the sauce requires and has never recreated her mother's decadent delight.

It was this friend who inspired me to invent a deconstructed mole, not so much because of her love for the sauce, but because of a story she recently shared. On a visit to a slightly seedy Mexican hole-in-the-wall, she decided to indulge for the first time in years in the chocolaty musk of mole negro. Knowing the dish could never surpass her mother's home-cooked handiwork she kept expectations low. But when the chile-spiked bowl of steaming chocolate stew arrived at the table, she was overcome, not with memories but with a new sensation—a tingling slightly south of the stomach. She turned to her husband, a consummate gourmet with a taste for ethnic cuisine, and felt her mouth form the words, "Are you thinking what I'm thinking?" Her husband could only nod—and smile. Can my rendition even come close? The proof is in the pudding, or in this case, the sauce.

hard sauce

Made with the scraped pods of tropical vanilla beans, this intense, creamy, white sauce works with pound cake, brownies, bread pudding, or simple fresh-picked fruit. You can substitute 1/2 t pure, liquid vanilla extract, but I can't guarantee the results.

preparation

Beat butter until light and fluffy, about 2 minutes. Sift confectioners' sugar into the butter. Split the vanilla bean in half and gently scrape seeds into the bowl, then add the liquor.

Beat in electric mixer on full speed for 5 minutes or until creamy.

Serve over cake, or cover and refrigerate. Bring to room temperature before using.

1/4 c butter, softened
3/4 c confectioners' sugar
seeds from 1/2 vanilla
bean, (approximately 4" of slender
bean).
1 T dark rum

sauces & libations

finding love the hard way

My mother grew up in the 50s on a comes-from-a-can diet. She did not discover the allure of pure vanilla until she traded in her parents' pantry for dormitory life and a college kitchen stocked with perishable goods. Vanilla-spiked hard sauce became her absolute favorite food during her freshman year. She would have devoured it by the vat if only the dining room staff could make enough to satisfy her desire—I would like to add, that freshman year was the same year she met my dad.

a word on wine

Wine is aphrodisiac. There it is. In a nutshell.

But if you don't buy my declaration, I can offer you an explanation. In a scientific setting, the aromas of wine have been found to replicate human pheromones (those nifty little receptors that communicate attraction to the brain). More specifically, several styles of wine including yeasty Champagnes, especially those decadently expensive vintage bottles, dry Rieslings, and the occasional Chardonnay, have been observed to replicate female pheromones. Earthy Pinot Noirs, burly Cabernet Sauvignons, and Bordeaux blends are the wines most often cited as replicating male pheromones. Some of my recommendations are: For whites, Bollinger Champagne—it worked for James Bond! (Champagne), Taittinger Compte de Champagne (Champagne), Tin Shed Wild Bunch Eden Valley Riesling (South Australia), and Tandem Sangiacomo Chardonnay (Russian River Valley). And in red wine, I reach for: Joseph Drouhin Beaune Clos des Mouches (Burgundy),

sauces & libations

Dehlinger Pinot Noir (Russian River Valley), Swanson Vineyards Alexis (Napa Valley), Chateaux Haut-Marbuzet (Bordeaux), Darioush Red Table Wine (Napa Valley), and Rejadorada Tinto Roble (Spain).

Although this means that hitting the right bottle may seriously improve your odds for romance whenever consuming alcohol, I recommend weighing carefully the wise words of William Shakespeare who suggested that alcohol "provokes the desire but takes away the performance."

a paragraph on port

When talking wine, the style I hear people classify as aphrodisiac more than any other wine is Port, the rich, sweet nectar made from fortified wine in Portugal's Douro Valley. Although little scientific information exists to support the assertion, it takes nothing more than a close look at Port's attributes to understand the sensual power of this ancient elixir. Even in its production, Port supports all that is lustful in the ancient art of wine production. Harvest in the Douro Valley is well documented as a Bacchanalian event with foot trodding to release the juice from the fruit's taut skin and dancing in the juice of the half-crushed grapes, coupled with late-night celebrations in the balmy autumn air. The aromas of Port almost without exception mimic most of the world's potent aphrodisiacs, including several of the stars of this book: honey, vanilla, and almonds (as well as cashews, hazelnuts, raspberries and licorice). My favorite producer, Taylor Fladgate, offers wines that often exhibit an aroma of violets, the scent ancient Greek women would use to perfume their vaginas for an edge in the game of attraction.

more potent elixirs

Although all alcohol has obvious effects of social lubrication, most spirits alone plainly don't produce amorous results. (It should be noted that a British study found alcohol to raise testosterone in women, but alas, not enough to have an arousing effect except those with the lowest of sex drives.) The exceptions are those distilled drinks containing thujone. Thujone is a narcotic; it comes from wormwood, a perennial plant that grows around the world. The most celebrated liquid made with wormwood is absinthe, more affectionately dubbed the green fairy.

absinthe

Absinthe, an emerald green potion with an aroma not unlike some old-fashioned tummy meds, was the drink of choice in the heyday of bohemian Paris. The period often gets credit for what was one of the most artistically and sexually free eras in Western history because its drinkers were drawn into a world of beautiful hallucinations. Sadly, today thujone is classified as a poison by the U.S. government. It is forbidden to import any absinthe made with wormwood into the country, and although there are a few thujone-free absinthes on the market, there really is no reason to bother. A word of warning: If you do stumble upon the illicit elixir, absinthe brings pleasure at a painful price. It is considered one of the most addictive drinks around and can be a catalyst for erratic behavior (Remember Vincent Van Gogh?).

sauces & libations

vermouth

Vermouth, it should be added, has earned martinis an aphrodisiac reputation because wormwood is one of the ingredients of fine vermouth. But really, more of the credit for the martini's iconic status must go to Sean Connery than to thujone, because the percentage of thujone in vermouth is immeasurable in order to allow the liquor legality.

layered experience

As a general rule, spirits used in seduction are best served layered with aphrodisiac ingredients. Here are several suggestions for elixirs of seduction (many of which have served me well).

magic mint syrup

I call this syrup "magic" because it makes everything taste so very good. I pour it on fruit salads, use it to sweeten lemonade, and douse mixed drinks with this syrup. It adds intensity to your basic mojito and is the perfect base for the Southern sweetheart of drinks, the mint julep.

preparation

1 c sugar
1 c water
1 1/2 c packed fresh
   mint leaves,
   coarsely chopped

In a small saucepan bring sugar, water, and mint to a boil, stirring until sugar is dissolved. Let your syrup gently simmer, undisturbed, for 2 minutes. Pour syrup through a fine sieve to remove the leaves. Cool before storing in the refrigerator.

Syrup keeps covered in the refrigerator for weeks.

some of my favorite uses

magic mint julep

preparation

Fill a pitcher with ice. Add cooled mint syrup, bourbon and stir. Pour into iced glasses and top with fresh mint sprigs.

Serving note: The magic mint julep tastes best served in traditional, silver mint julep cups.

1 c magic mint syrup
1 c bourbon
sprigs of fresh mint for
garnish

magic mint lemonade

preparation

Combine the 2 cups of water and the sugar in a medium sauce pot. Bring to a boil and cook just until the sugar is dissolved. Cool to room temperature.

Combine 1/2 c mint syrup, sugar water, and lemon juice in a pitcher and chill.

Serve over ice. (Tastes best sucked through a straw.)

1/2 c magic mint syrup
2 c water
1/3 c sugar*
3/4 c fresh lemon juice
2 tall glasses filled with
ice

*Substitute Splenda for
a low-sugar version.

sauces & libations

white peach Bellini

by Master Mixologist Tony Abou-Ganim

The Bellini is one of the world's most classic drinks of seduction. It was created in Venice, the city of romance, but its heady combination of sweet peach and Champagne fizz is notorious around the world.

preparation

FOR THE PURÉE:
1 lb very ripe white peaches
2 T fresh lemon juice
fresh red raspberries (optional)
extra sugar to taste
2 oz fresh white peach purée
3 oz Prosecco sparkling wine
2 chilled Champagne flutes

Begin by making peach purée: fill a large stock pot with water and bring to a boil. Blanch peaches in boiling water for approximately 1 minute and transfer to an ice bath. Peel peaches and remove stones. Purée peaches in a food processor adding 1/2 oz fresh lemon juice for each peach. Sweeten to taste if needed, approximately 1 oz of sugar per pound of peaches. (*Hint:* Add a couple of red raspberries for color.)

In the mixing glass of a Boston shaker, add ice, 2 oz peach purée and 3 oz chilled Prosecco, roll the drink between the mixing glass and shaker tin to blend—do NOT shake. Strain into a chilled Champagne flute. (If you do not have a mixing glass, pour the Prosecco directly into your chilled flute then top with the peach purée. But if you plan on making Bellinis a habit, invest in the best equipment. The pouring method will not as thoroughly integrate the ingredients.)

my Bellini bliss

I am a sucker for a great Bellini, but I've never been able to make one myself. So I called upon Tony Abu Ganim, one of my favorite tastemakers, (who also happens to be among the best barmen in the world). Tony's secret starts with fresh, white peaches, the riper the better. A consummate bartender, Tony never spills, so I don't know how well the drink has ever helped him score, but as for me...the way to a woman's heart just may be through the Bellini.

sauces & libations

saffron fleurtation

by Liz Dueland, public relations director for Perrier Jouët, bubble babe and sensualist extraordinaire

In many parts of the world, saffron is associated with fertility, particularly in reference to wedding celebrations. In our culture, there is no Champagne linked more with bridal celebration than Perrier Jouët Fleur de Champagne, the wine best recognized by the bridal white bouquet etched on the face of its bottle.

It probably doesn't surprise you to hear that we aphrodisiac addicts stick together, which is how Liz Dueland fell into my life. Dueland thinks of her wine not as a bridal banquet staple but as the imbibe-able embodiment of flirtation—or as she calls it, fleurtation.

preparation

1 bottle Perrier Jouët Fleur de Champagne*
20 saffron threads, toasted

*Substitute any high quality, vintage brut Champagne

Crush 5 saffron threads in each of two Champagne flutes. Top with Champagne and toast to the art of flirtation. Drain and repeat.

feelings from a flirt, by Liz

On par with Casanova's mystique, Champagne is an ultimate aphrodisiac. Because of the bubbles, it enters the blood stream more quickly than other spirits and initiates a romantic evening from the first sip. However, it typically has less alcohol than still wine, so you are always alert and ready for all the evening's wonderful events to unfold.

Let the bubbles tickle the nose and raise awareness of all the senses.

In this specific cocktail, a few threads of saffron add layers of complexity to the already floral and biscuity Perrier Jouët. Added to its impact is saffron's lore. In preparing this drink for a feast aux deux, I like to recall how it was used by the ancient Phoenicians as a love spice to flavor the moon-shaped cake eaten in honor of Ashtoreth, the goddess of fertility. For me, it is not just a drink of romance but is also the ideal honeymoon libation…the cocktail to use as the mating call begins.

a very sexy cocktail

a variation on a creation by Mixologist Tony Abou-Ganim that is served at the Sushi Roku restaurants in Los Angeles and Las Vegas

1 1/2 oz fig flavored
    vodka (I like
    Feigling)
3/4 oz Marie Brizard
    Cassis de Bordeaux
1 1/2 oz fresh lemon
    sour mix*
Brut Champagne

*Mixing two parts freshly squeezed, filtered lemon juice with one part simple syrup will easily make fresh sour mix. Adding a dollop of egg white will give your drink a rich, creamy head.

FOR GARNISH:
1 T each small raspberries and blackberries
Grand Marnier
4 small mission figs
1 egg white
fine sugar

According to Tony Abou-Ganim, this drink's sexiest element is the "big finish." Nothing could be more festive or fitting than a topping of Champagne to bring a cocktail to life—from the cork's release to the rush of tiny bubbles, this quintessential celebratory libation never fails to infuse that added element of cheer. Needless to say for this drink, only "very sexy" Champagnes need apply.

preparation

In an ice filled shaker add vodka, cassis, and fresh sour; shake until well blended. Strain into a chilled cocktail glass with marinated berries and top with a splash of Champagne. Serve presented on a small saucer with one perfect, candied fig.

FOR THE BERRIES:
Marinate red raspberries and blackberries in superfine sugar and Grand Marnier. Set aside.

FOR THE FIGS:
Dip each fig in egg white and sprinkle with fine sugar. Dry figs in an oven on the lowest setting for 30 minutes. Cool until hard, at least 1 hour.

sauces & libations

The pro's perspective from master mixologist Tony Abou-Ganim

Why did I make a drink dubbed "very sexy?" Synonymous with the somewhat overused and frequently inadequate idiom, "the best," very sexy is used in the culinary world to declare an object or creation of utmost perfection. For example, "Those are some very sexy mushrooms," or "His steak frites are very sexy," or in this case, "That is one very sexy cocktail."

honey drop

*by Todd Bellucci, white-hot Hollywood
drinks consultant*

This sinful shooter begins with a touch of spice on the lips, a bite of citrus on the tongue, and finishes with a sweet coating of honey. Todd created the drink for a feature I was writing on honey, and although the story is long gone, the drink is a keeper.

preparation

FOR THE RIM:
1/2 t chile powder
1/2 t salt
honey

Mix chile and salt in a shallow dish. Dip rim in honey and roll in the chile and salt.

Pour vodka and lime juice into shot glass. Top with a drop of honey.

FOR THE SHOOTER:
1 oz vodka
1 oz fresh squeezed lime
    juice
honey to taste

behind the bar with Bellucci

There's something to be said for the sweet and heat combo—it seems to work particularly well on women. Sweetness is a common thread in aphrodisiac foods, but the addition of spice seems to shed inhibitions.

Repeat as often as necessary.

bloody Maria

This drink's true potency comes from its heat. The usual Tabasco is replaced with ancho chile powder to give Maria a naughty little kick.

preparation

Combine all the ingredients in a pitcher and mix well. Fill a tall glass with ice and drench ice with the tequila mixture. Garnish with a lime wedge and serve with a smile.

8 oz tomato juice
2 oz tequila
1 T lime juice
dash Worcestershire
    sauce
1 t ancho chile powder
1/2 t garlic salt
fresh lime for garnish

a tale of tequila

In reality, it was the worm in the bottle that supposedly made tequila an aphrodisiac. Yet I cling to the tradition of tequila itself as an aphrodisiac (though you can bet I drink my hooch worm-free). Not to say that I think tequila has any more ability to arouse than vodka, but I prefer the bite it brings to the basic Bloody Mary.

ginger mojito

3 sprigs fresh mint
1 1/2 lime
1 T ginger syrup*
1 1/2 oz light rum
3 oz club soda
fresh-made ice (Ice
    that's been sticking
    around in your
    freezer will make
    your drink taste like
    the freezer.)

*I use Robert Lambert
White Ginger Syrup, but
for something homemade:
1 c sugar
1 c water
1/4 c coarsely chopped
    fresh ginger root

The Mojito is a Cuban classic, made popular in the steamy bars of Havana in the mid-20th century. It is a red-hot drink made by combining fresh citrus with the sweet heat of rum. My version takes a twist on the original by adding the bite of ginger. Although the flavor is not traditional, this version is a drink that makes me want to kiss.

preparation

Crush half the mint at the bottom of a chilled, tall glass. (If you want to get serious with your mint, get a muddler, a bartender's baton that looks

like a mini billy club, but a homemade muddler...
I am talking about a big spoon...will do the trick.)
Blend juice, syrup and rum; top with club soda,
cool off with ice, and garnish with a mint sprig.

FOR THE GINGER SYRUP:

Get sugar, water, and ginger hot in a small
sauce pan. Once sugar is dissolved, gently boil
for 8–10 minutes or until the syrup has reduced
by a little more than half, to produce about 2/3
cup.

Cool completely in the refrigerator. Strain
ginger from syrup before serving.

Cuban cravings

I love traditional mojitos. But why not do it
one better? Rum already teases with some heat,
and that extra layer brought on by the ginger
pushes me over the edge.

dessert

chocolate smothered brie
chocolate

creamy vanilla shakes with
malted milk ball rims
vanilla

fresh figs rolled in brown sugar
fig

ready for anything
ginger piecrust
ginger

easy mango tart tatin
mango

Persian love cake
saffron

cranberry almond tart
almond

make whoopee pie
chocolate

breakfast in bed triple gingerbread
ginger

morning after fig scones
with fresh cream
fig

chocolate smothered brie

I've noticed that sometimes there is a disparity between the kind of pleasure women and men find in food.

This one's for the ladies.

Both chocolate and cheese, the recipe's two main ingredients, contain phenylethylamine, PEA, a chemical believed to aid in stimulating sexual arousal—good for both men and women. But soft, ripe brie emits an aroma that is said to trigger pheromone receptors in women, making this dish ladies' choice.

preparation

2 cloves garlic, thinly
    sliced
1 1/2 t butter
1 1/2 c dark chocolate
    chips
1/2 c heavy cream
6 oz wedge of ripe brie
1 pint strawberries,
    washed with stems
    on
1/2 French baguette

Put garlic on a baking tray and sprinkle chunks of butter on top. Toast under the broiler until just brown. (Adult supervision recommended.) Remove from broiler and toss the hard, golden chips in the melted butter and set aside to rest.

Arrange the brie and strawberries on a serving platter.

In a double boiler or a metal mixing bowl fitted onto a small pot of simmering water, gently melt the chocolate chips with the cream over low heat, stirring steadily with a gentle motion. (*Note:* You can melt chocolate in the microwave, but it burns very easily. Only try this method if you feel sure of your technique.)

Desserts

When chocolate reaches a smooth, creamy texture, remove from heat and fold in the hard garlic chips.

Smother the cheese with the hot chocolate and allow the sweet topping to drench a few berries.

Serve immediately with a hunk of French bread and a total lack of inhibition.

from the layperson's perspective

My friend Juli declares this dish to be "better than sex." For the record, I don't think she would live a life devoid of sex in exchange for melted chocolate and brie, but this dish definitely hits a girl with a wash of happy hormones.

desserts

creamy vanilla shakes
with malted milk ball rims

What can I really say about a milkshake? It's creamy, smooth, nutritious, and delicious.

preparation

1 c vanilla ice cream or frozen yogurt
1 c milk or, for a thick shake, half-and-half

1 t vanilla extract
4-5 malted milk balls, crushed

Dip the lip of two glasses in a saucer of milk. Then dip into a dish of crushed milk balls while rolling the lip gently to coat with chocolate dust.

In a blender, combine ice cream, milk and vanilla extract. Blend until smooth. Pour the frothy shakes carefully into the milk ball rimmed glasses and drink immediately.

my milkshakes

Some fans of my milkshake have a serving suggestion for taking the sucking experience to a whole new level. Try alternately sucking the creamy shake through a straw and licking the chocolate from the rim.

desserts   113

fresh figs rolled in brown sugar

I love to play with my food. Sharing the experience and getting my hands involved in the game brings a spark of excitement and creativity. And besides, who doesn't love a roll in the... sugar?

preparation

Serve sour cream and brown sugar in separate bowls. Dip figs in the cream and then roll in the sugar.

6 fresh figs, quartered
1/4 c sour cream
2 T brown sugar

ready for anything ginger piecrust

by Chef Ivy Haaks, creator of Whole Haute organic delivery in Los Angeles

This candied crust dances in perfect harmony with many sensual fruits—let your imagination run wild. It is superb filled with passion fruit mousse or simply piled with slices of rich

desserts

ripe mangoes and strawberries. Lemon or lime custard filling makes a perfect combination of hot, sweet and tart.

Give yourself enough time to prepare the pie or tart in advance and be sure to let the filling chill for a couple of hours. Then serve this dessert to someone who deserves your undivided attention and let the evening's adventure unfold.

preparation

2 T crystallized ginger, finely chopped
1/4 c confectioner's sugar
1 1/2 c all purpose, unbleached white flour
8 T cold butter, cut into small cubes
1 egg yolk
2 T cold water

Blend the crystallized ginger, sugar and flour in a medium bowl. Add butter. Either using an electric mixer or a pastry cutter, combine the mixture until you have a crumbly texture. Add in the egg yolk and 1 tablespoon of water. Beat it to a sticky dough. If the mixture is too dry, lubricate with the second tablespoon of water and mix again until your dough comes together. Let the dough rest covered in the refrigerator for one hour.

When you remove the dough from the refrigerator, let it stand at room temperature for about 10 minutes. Sprinkle a clean, dry work surface (preferably marble) with flour. Using a rolling pin, flatten the dough into a circle.

Preheat oven to 350 degrees.

Spray a 9-inch pie plate with non-stick cooking spray. Line the pan with the rolled and cut pastry and trim the top edges to meet the rim of the pan. Place the tart shell in the freezer for

Desserts

about 30 minutes. When crust has chilled, place a piece of parchment paper on top of the pastry dough and layer dried beans on top of the crust. (This will weigh down the pastry and prevent the crust from having unwanted bulges that tend to grow as the crust gets hot.)

Bake the pastry at 350 degrees for about 15 minutes until the tart shell begins to brown. Remove the parchment paper with the beans and bake the naked shell for an additional 10 minutes or until the tart is golden. Let the crust cool to room temperature before adding your favorite creamy filling to the tart.

Ivy's secret ingredient

I use ginger for its warming, stimulating effect. Making the ginger piecrust is just the thing to arouse inner heat at the end of a luscious meal. It brings a natural blush to my face as its heat takes effect. The recipe calls for crystallized ginger, which I think is perfect for experiencing the root's mouth-watering sweetness mixed with its powerful warmth.

easy mango tart tatin

In my estimation, mango is a nearly perfect food. But if there is one thing that can improve this gift of nature, it would have to be sweet, creamery butter. Although this easy variation on a traditional French tart makes servings for eight, I once served this tart to a group of four who devoured the entire caramel-tinged pie in minutes.

preparation

4 T unsalted butter, cut into small slices
1/2 c sugar
1 1/2 ripe mangoes, peeled, pitted and thinly sliced
1 frozen puff pastry sheet
whipped cream *optional

Preheat oven to 400 degrees.

Lubricate bottom of tart pan or 10-inch glass pie pan with butter. Be sure to rub the sides of the pan. Then drop remaining butter in bottom of pan. Sprinkle sugar on top of the butter. Layer the thin mango slices in a fan pattern on top of your hot sugar. Lay the sheet of pastry over your ripe fruit. Trim the pastry and then tuck the edges inside the rim of the pan. Bake for 20–25 minutes, until crust is golden brown.

Let hot tart cool for 10 minutes.

After cooling slightly, slide an inverted serving platter over the top of the tart. Using hot pads (your tart will still be sizzling to the touch) flip the sandwiched tart so that the platter is on the bottom. Slide the pan off the top gently, so as not to disturb your cooling fruit.

desserts

Preheat broiler and move oven rack to top row. Broil tart, about 4 minutes, until sugars begin to caramelize on your thinly sliced fruit and the top turns golden. Watch your tart carefully to avoid burning edges.

Slice and serve with a kiss of whipped cream.

butter baby

Nothing beats the taste and crunch of sugar caramelized with butter. I find it especially magical when mingled with the soft, sweet flesh of tropical mango. If you're looking for the quintessential sexy food, this just might be the definitive dessert, or at least, the perfect prelude to it.

desserts

Persian love cake
with candied rose petals

Iranian culture embraces many traditions that involve both food and romance. As a matter of fact, small slices of Persian wedding cake are traditionally brought home by mothers to their little girls (who are not generally permitted at Iranian weddings), to bring them luck in finding true love some day.

This recipe is not a traditional Persian wedding cake. It is simply a visually stunning cake that showcases some of the region's most exotic aphrodisiac flavors. A touch of saffron in the icing brings a warm buttercream hue to a whipped-cream white frosting, but it is the intensity of the cardamom in the cake's moist interior that makes this pretty little sweet a feast to remember.

Cardamom is an ancient Eastern spice somewhat unfamiliar in Western cooking. We usually see it in a ground powder, if at all. But it is worth seeking out the unground seeds (you probably will have to purchase them in whole pods and remove the tiny seeds by hand). Tasting almost like an intense combination of ginger, cinnamon and anise, it is the cardamom that brings tiny palate-teasing explosions of flavor to the cake.

Although it adds an extra step of preparation and several hours drying time, you'll want to be sure to make the candied rose decoration. Not

Desserts

only do the sugared rose petals bring extraordinary beauty to the final cake, but they also lend a sweet shock of flavor to every slice.

preparation

Preheat oven to 325 degrees.

Butter two 8 x 1 1/2 inch cake pans. Prepare cake batter according to mix instructions. Add lemon zest and cardamom and mix thoroughly. Divide between the 2 prepared pans and cook according to package instructions. Cool in pans on racks 15 minutes. Turn out onto racks and cool completely.

1 vanilla cake mix
eggs and oil as called for in cake mix directions
1 t grated lemon zest
2 t whole cardamom seeds

FOR THE FROSTING:

Combine 1/2 cup cream and saffron in small saucepan and heat to a simmer. Remove from heat, letting steep 20 minutes. Chill until cold.

Beat remaining 2 cups cream, powdered sugar and rose water in large bowl until soft peaks form. Strain chilled saffron cream and add to whipped cream. Beat until you've formed stiff peaks, then fold in cream cheese.

FOR THE FROSTING:
2 1/2 c chilled heavy whipping cream
pinch of saffron threads
2/3 c powdered sugar
3/4 t rose water
2 T cream cheese

TO ASSEMBLE:

Place 1 cake layer, flat side up, on platter. Spread 1 cup frosting over layer. Top with second cake layer, flat side down. Spread remaining frost-

Desserts

ing over top and sides of cake. Chill at least 1 hour and up to 6 hours. Garnish cake with rose petals.

FOR THE CANDIED ROSE
PETALS
(prepare at least 6 hours
in advance):
2 large egg whites
1/2 c sugar
petals from 2 brightly
colored organic
roses

TO MAKE CANDIED ROSE PETALS:
Whisk egg whites in small bowl until foamy. Using pastry brush, brush rose petals on both sides with egg whites; sprinkle both sides with sugar. Dry on nonstick rack at least 6 hours or overnight.

rose to the occasion

Both sexy and sophisticated, this rose-covered confection is the kind of cake I like to make for special occasions like anniversaries or an intimate wedding. Though I'll make the cake for a crowd, I always like to take my piece home to serve with two forks.

desserts

cranberry almond tart

This is a variation of an old *Life of Reiley* family recipe from Cape Cod. Despite the cold winter nights of New England, this tart is truly hot.

Although I can speak with confidence about the aphrodisiac properties of almonds, I have friends, cranberry bog owners as a matter of fact, who swear by the aphrodisiac power of cranberries. And judging by the fact that they've been happily married for over thirty years, I should think they know best.

preparation

Get your oven hot, 325 degrees to be exact.

Lay cranberries on bottom of a well-greased 10" pie pan. Top with 1/2 cup of sugar and your nuts.

In a medium size bowl, beat eggs until they are just frothy. Slowly, rhythmically, stir in the sugar and whip until completely mixed. Add the flour, butter and milk, and beat it some more.

Top berries with creamy egg batter and bake for 1 hour in your hot oven. Serve warm. (Tart serves 8.)

FOR THE FILLING:
2 c fresh or frozen cranberries
1/2 c sugar
1/2 c chopped almonds

FOR THE BATTER:
2 eggs
1 c sugar
1 c flour
1/2 c butter, melted
1/3 c milk

desserts

it's so easy

How can something so simple be so satisfying? Ten minutes of prep for an hour of blissful anticipation. When this sweet pie's aromas begin to invade every corner of the house, you will start to understand just how little effort can bring sinful reward.

make whoopee pie

This do-it-yourself sensual exploration is like a childhood fantasy sundae bar turned sinfully sweet. And it is best enjoyed as a shared experience between four hands and two tongues.

I created this variation of a Pennsylvania Dutch mainstay somewhat by accident. Traditional whoopee pies are made with a vegetable shortening filling, but I wanted to create an icing with all-natural butter instead. I could never seem to get my cream filling stiff enough, (I know...the irony!) but where there's a will there's a way, and I finally found I was able to bring my icing to perfect stiffness by chilling it—until I was ready to serve some whoopee.

preparation

Preheat oven to 350 degrees.

In a medium bowl, combine flour, cocoa, baking soda and salt. Set aside.

In a separate bowl, mix together the sugar and eggs until fluffy. Add the vanilla.

Add 1/3 of the dry ingredients to your wet mixture, and then add 1/3 of the buttermilk. Continue alternating until everything is incorporated.

Drop batter by small mounds on cookie sheets to form 16 rounded cookies. Bake for 12-15 minutes, until center is firm.

Melt butter with marshmallows over low heat. Remove from heat and stir remaining ingredients into the white cream. Beat until fluffy. Spread between whoopee pie cookies to form cream-filled sandwiches.

1 3/4 c flour
1/2 c dark cocoa
1 t baking soda
1/2 t salt
3/4 c sugar
1 egg
1/2 t pure vanilla extract
1/2 c buttermilk

FOR THE FILLING:
3 T butter
2 marshmallows
1 1/4 c powdered sugar
1 egg white
pods scraped from 1
    whole vanilla bean
    or 1 t pure vanilla
    extract

desserts

going all the way

For this dessert to work, you have to invest a little physical effort. Your reward will be a multi-level sensory experience. First, there's the flirtation of dipping and spreading together that becomes deliciously messy, thanks to the marshmallow. Spreading the icing allows you to choose how thick you want to spread the cream on your cookie and delivers a heady hit of vanilla as you work. (Don't forget, vanilla historically is used as an aid in raising more than expectations.) The layers of warm cookie and cold icing surprise the tongue with opposing sensations. The cookies can be made ahead, but how could you pass up the promise of frosting-on-frosting action?

breakfast in bed
triple gingerbread

This is the best gingerbread I've ever had.
Yes, I eat it in bed.

preparation

Preheat oven to 350 degrees.

Grease and flour an 8 1/2 x 4 1/2 inch loaf pan. Mix the first 4 ingredients in a medium bowl. Add 3 tablespoons crystallized ginger.

Beat the butter and both sugars in large bowl until the mixture becomes light and frothy. Beat in eggs, 1 egg at a time. Mix in fresh ginger.

Stir the dry ingredients into the creamed butter and egg mixture, alternating with buttermilk, beginning and ending with dry ingredients.

Transfer batter to waiting pan. Sprinkle remaining 3 T crystallized ginger over batter.

Bake until a toothpick, gently inserted into the cake's warm center, comes out clean, about 50 minutes.

Turn out onto rack and cool completely. Serve slices with vanilla yogurt and a bowl of just washed strawberries.

1 1/2 c all purpose flour
1 t ground ginger
1 t ground cinnamon
1 t baking soda
6 T crystallized ginger, minced
1/2 c (1 stick) unsalted butter, room temperature
1/2 c packed brown sugar
1/3 c sugar
2 large eggs
3 T ginger, peeled and grated)
1/2 c buttermilk

desserts

breaking all the rules

Although my parents never imposed such silly policies, as a child I recall that most of my friends were not allowed to eat in bed. If you were among the gastronomically repressed, now is the time to grow up and move on. There's nothing better than snuggling down between the sheets and nibbling a big chunk of sweet, hot ginger.

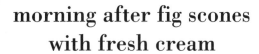

morning after fig scones with fresh cream

*by Chef Sondra Bernstein, author, proprietress of
The Girl and The Fig Restaurant and
wild wine country woman*

Sondra Bernstein, who founded The Girl and The Fig Restaurant in Sonoma, California, shared this recipe with me. Sondra, a woman who managed to build a career around the seduction of figs, uses them here to their utmost capacity. The fig's punch of sexually stimulating nutrients

desserts

is coupled with sweet jam and whipped cream in a treat truly fitting for a morning in bed.

RECIPE NOTES:

Use cold butter for the shortbread scones, and don't overwork the dough.

It is okay to use store-bought jam ("The Girl and The Fig" Black Mission Fig Jam is Sondra's choice).

preparation

Roughly chop figs and cook with the sugar and thyme over medium heat, stirring constantly until fruits are thick and tender (approximately 15 to 20 minutes). Remove thyme and slowly, with a steady rhythm, stir in lemon zest and juice.

Preheat oven to 350 degrees.

In a large bowl, stir together flour, baking powder, sugar and salt. Cut in butter with a pastry cutter using a slicing motion to create a consistency like coarse breadcrumbs. Stir in dried figs.

In a separate bowl, whisk together egg and milk. Stir into flour mixture a bit at a time until just mixed.

On a clean, floured countertop, pat dough out to 1-inch thickness. Using a 2-inch round cookie cutter, cut into scones. Place the cut dough on a buttered and lightly floured baking sheet. (If you don't have a cookie cutter, you can

FIG JAM
Makes 1 quart
2 1/2 lb ripe figs
1/4 c sugar
several sprigs fresh
    thyme
1 large lemon, juice and
    zest

FOR THE SCONES:
Makes 6 scones
1 1/2 c all purpose flour
1 1/2 t baking powder
1 1/2 t granulated sugar
1 pinch salt
1/2 c cold butter, cut
    into chunks
1/2 c diced dried figs
1 egg
1/2 c milk

desserts

FOR THE EGG WASH:
1 egg
2 T milk

FOR THE FIG SYRUP:
1 c fig jam
2 c Port wine
1/2 c sugar
1 vanilla bean

FOR THE TOPPING:
1 c whipped cream
1 t granulated sugar

shape your scones by hand.) Re-roll scraps and cut into scones until all the scraps are gone.

Make the egg wash by whisking together the egg and milk. Using a pastry brush, brush egg wash over unbaked scones.

Bake for 20 minutes or until scones are golden. Remove immediately from tray and cool on a wire rack.

FOR THE FIG SYRUP:

In a pot, combine jam, Port, sugar and vanilla bean. Reduce by 2/3. Strain.

Gently fold sugar into whipped cream and chill until ready to eat.

Drizzle fig syrup on plate, fingers and lover. Cut scone in half lengthwise, spread fig jam on your bottom piece, add whipped cream, and top with your second scone slice. Top with a voluptuous dollop of whipped cream and commence licking, nibbling and, when you can't resist any longer, unbridled devouring.

Sunday and Sondra

My perfect Sunday morning: a light rain shower that results in a rainbow, silky pajamas, fresh-squeezed mimosas, cafe lattes, Sunday cartoons, Chopin's Waltz in B minor, foot massages, and fig scones with whipped cream and fig syrup.

Desserts

venues

kitchen: the new bedroom

In our world of sexual repression and food-inspired double entendre, the kitchen is the new bedroom. It is the room that contains all the necessary cooking equipment—in many of our homes, that includes a delightful array of shiny toys. And it is a domain filled with creative and surprisingly sexual delights.

For someone like me who can't help but link passion and food, the kitchen is a natural starting line for playing games of love. But if the thought of fooling around to the pilot light still sounds awkward to you, chew on this: Dr. Alan Hirsch of the Smell and Taste Treatment and Research Foundation in Chicago, a scientific researcher fascinated by the human body's subconscious reactions to aromas, discovered that culinary scents can be among the most sexually arousing smells in the world.

An almost sure bet for seducing a man is to tease his senses with a stock pot of water scented with lavender and pumpkin pie spice simmering on the stovetop. This combination of scents is shown to be one of the most arousing stimulants to men.

And if you thought the link between women and cucumbers was all just a dirty joke left over from your teens, think again. For women, there are few smells more sexually arousing than that of the slender green fruit. One of this book's starring foods is among the most desired scents by both men and women—the soothing smell of vanilla—the ultimate aroma for evoking emotions associated with comfort, security and home.

Even if you choose to move (probably wisely) to more comfortable quarters before commencing more acrobatic pursuits, try playing in the kitchen as a backdrop to seduction.

Recipes for sparking passion by the pilot light:
hard tacos with hot guacamole (pg 75)
dipping green goddess (pg 81)
make whoopee pies (pg 123)

Dining room

According to experts on etiquette, table manners represent the ultimate tools of power and persuasion. Some authorities even tout table manners as the sharpest weapons in a societal version of warfare fought among social classes.

Can the way you hold a fork truly influence your position of power in society? Remember the story of the magazine editor I mentioned who was seduced over mangos and chocolate? It was not only the ingredients that sailed her down the river of love. Just consider the scene we almost always select for sexual negotiations. In the hunt for romance, "crucial" dates, like the second and third, generally take place in a dining room, whether in a restaurant or your home. And there, over the formal dining table, the most sweetly agonizing dance of seduction begins. Those gratifying struggles to maintain perfect composure while rocked by the force of attraction (a power that grows by the minute the longer a meal lasts) have created the memories at the foundation of my most rewarding romantic relationships.

Recipes for traditional foreplay:
green tea poached salmon (pg 66)
chocolate smothered brie (pg 111)
fresh figs rolled in brown sugar (pg 114)

venues

roaring fire

The smell of a crackling fire does wonders for my appetite. Yes, I know, romance in front of a roaring fire is totally cliché, but think back to a point touched on earlier in this book—that clichés become so for a reason. And for me, at least, this cliché works because of the pleasure of the foods associated with an open fire.

Many of my favorite aphrodisiac foods taste best cooked over an open fire: chicken apple sausages, chestnuts, suckling pig, and of course, marshmallows. Try roasting marshmallows and feeding them stuffed with dark chocolate chips to your lover by the light of a flickering fire.

Recipes for fireside romance:
hot honey nuts (pg 39)
love linguine with almond pesto (pg 59)
saffron fleurtation (pg 101)

bath tub

I have not read any research on the effects of eating in the bath, but I do know that bathing is considered one of the most sensual overtures to romance. And to me, gastronomy is a natural mate to bubbles, bodies, and utter indulgence.

When I was working at my first job in the culinary industry with a Northern California winery, I liked to unwind by coming home and savoring a glass of wine in a long hot bubble bath. Adding a box of chocolates to the mix, I'd let the explosion of flavors wash over me. It was an incredible act of indulgence and intimacy, the kind of personal act that reconnects you with your own body. And I've found that harmonizing with another body is at its most exciting when I'm totally in tune with my own needs.

I've also decided that calories consumed in the tub most definitely don't count.

Recipes for heating up the bath:
a very sexy cocktail (pg 103)
shrimp stuffed spring rolls (pg 47)
creamy milkshakes with
malted milkball rims (pg 113)

backyard

I am lucky enough to have a hammock built for two in my backyard. It takes an adventurer to risk the acrobatics of fooling around on this perch, but as a place to eat a deux, it is perfect.

Porch swings, hammocks and chaise lounges are all wonderful alternative dining spots. They are intimate and encourage sharing. The balancing act required by any one of these dining places heightens awareness and forces attention away from the external plagues on the mind and onto the pleasures of the food to be consumed.

There is just one trick that I have yet to master, and that is the balancing act to allow for simultaneous plate balancing, wine drinking and hand-holding.

Recipes for backyard cravings:

lamb burgers with my sweet
peach chutney (pg 69)

fire grilled chops with
horseradish-mint sauce (pg 77)

fruit salad drenched in
magic mint syrup (pg 97)

into the woods

A picnic is a perfect way to set a scene of seduction. The picnic of love, as I like to call it, is a classic scene in great works of literature and one whose indelible imagery carries over into film and television.

I think this Technicolor vision of picnics for two is what gives this romantic lure its recipe for success. I have never seen hard-core stats on the

subject, but I have heard that picnicking is now touted among the top "rekindling" tips for couples that complain of having lost that spark.

I've never actually been in a position to need picnicking to regain passion. But I do know that a romp in the grass definitely brings back memories of carefree teenage flings. Whether or not that one works for you, you'll have to discover for yourself. For me, the sensory experience of dining in the secluded outdoors is an aphrodisiac in itself.

Many of the smells of the wooded earth, like the carpet of wildflowers, brambles and damp, mossy wood are themselves associated with arousal, so imagine how enticing they can become when mingled with vintage Champagne, French bread and a wedge of ripe brie or hard, peppered salami. And, truth be told, there is always the element of excitement in that canoodling in any outdoor venue, no matter how secluded, risks discovery.

Recipes for splendor in the grass:
rosemary potato salad with fat sausages (pg 62)
white peach bellinis (pg 99)
Persian love cake (pg 119)

rocking the boat

It is nearly impossible to imagine anything with a more pure flavor than freshly caught seafood. Legend has it that Aphrodite, the goddess from whom aphrodisiacs get their name, was born of the sea and carried to land on the surf.

With the exception of those allergic to the fruits of the sea, everyone should have the experience of eating seafood plucked straight from the ocean.

Whether it's oysters plucked from their beds and shucked on a rowboat or sea bass line-caught from a sailing yacht and sautéed in rosemary butter down below, the combination of sea air, sun and fresh food is the sweetest sensory explosion.

Rocking a catamaran is one thing, but if you succumb to passion, you may want to row ashore if your boat is on the small, less accommodating side before indulging in earthly delights.

Recipes for romance at sea:
honey-almond home cured snapper (pg 49)
vanilla scented sea bass with
a red hot rub (pg 67)
ginger mojitos (pg 107)

bed

According to *The Joy of Sex*, the bed is still "the most important piece of domestic sexual equipment." To that I would like to add that it is an excellent place for intimate eating.

Breakfast in bed is considered one of the most indulgent domestic treats in our culture, but eating in bed need not be limited to the morning. Chocolate mint ice cream scooped straight from the carton will melt to the perfect, creamy consistency when snuggled between two bodies.

I've tried eating many of the dishes from this book in bed and can highly recommend nearly all of them. (One exception is the chocolate covered brie. I find that French bread leaves too many crumbs between the sheets.)

Recipes for pleasure in bed:
figs in a blanket (pg 41)
honey drop (pg 105)
easy mango tart tatin (pg 117)
breakfast in bed triple gingerbread (pg 126)

glossary

beat: to mix moist ingredients with short, rhythmic movements.

cream: to work butter into a smooth, soft paste.

fork: 1. a utensil with a long, slender handle and 3-4 sharp prongs. 2. to make something into a shape that connects at one end then branches into two.

meat thermometer: see probe thermometer.

pat: to touch repeatedly with light pressure using the palm of a hand, generally with the intention of shaping or smoothing.

press: to squeeze with the intention of releasing liquid.

probe thermometer: also called a meat thermometer, a probe thermometer is used to measure the internal temperature of hot, cooking meat.

roast: to coax a food into the perfect state of doneness through prolonged exposure to heat.

roll: 1. a delectable treat formed by wrapping one food, generally flesh, around a savory or sweet filling. 2. to move or shape with a repetitive turning or rotating motion.

rub: 1. a blend of spices applied by rubbing. 2. to make contact with a surface, moving hand with a repeated, purposeful motion.

simmer: to bring a food to the point of heat so that it bubbles gently, just below boiling.

soft peak: the stage at which a spoon inserted into whipped egg whites or a cream mixture will form peaks but still will be soft enough that the peaks will droop when the spoon is pulled out.

spoon: 1. a utensil with a shallow bowl attached to a long, slender handle, used for eating. 2. to mold your body to that of another from behind with affectionate or amorous intent.

squeeze: to manually exert pressure, usually in order to extract liquid.

stiff peak: the stage at which a spoon inserted into whipped egg whites or a cream mixture will form erect peaks after the spoon is pulled out.

whip: to beat a liquid into a state of froth with a steady and rhythmic motion.

glossary

recipe index

almond
honey-almond home cured snapper   49
love linguine with almond pesto   59
cranberry almond tart   122

chile
hot honey nuts   39
hard tacos with hot guacamole   75
chile rub   82
bloody Maria   106

chocolate
first time fluffernutters   42
not wholly mole   88
chocolate smothered brie   111
make whoopee pies   123

fig
figs in a blanket   41
a very sexy cocktail   103
fresh figs rolled in brown sugar   114
morning after fig scones with fresh cream   127

ginger
ginger mojito   107
ready for anything ginger piecrust   114
breakfast in bed triple gingerbread   126

honey
honey carrot soup   55
sweet and hot apricot sauce   86
honey drop   105

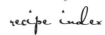

recipe index